PENGUIN B

THE BHAIS OF B

Jyoti Shelar is an award-winning journalist who has been covering crime, healthcare and communities for over a decade. Currently an assistant editor with *The Hindu*, she has previously worked with *Mumbai Mirror*, *Hindustan Times* and *DNA*. She has closely mapped developments in the public healthcare sector. Shelar is a fellow of the International Center for Journalists (ICFJ) and has also been a Thomson Reuters Foundation fellow. When not on the field, she enjoys kicking back with a paperback or binge watching American sitcoms.

THE **BHAIS** OF **BENGALURU**

Foreword by S. Hussain Zaidi

JYOTI SHELAR

BLUE SALT

PENGUIN BOOKS

An imprint of Penguin Random House

PENGUIN BOOKS

USA | Canada | UK | Ireland | Australia
New Zealand | India | South Africa | China

Penguin Books is part of the Penguin Random House group of companies
whose addresses can be found at global.penguinrandomhouse.com

Published by Penguin Random House India Pvt. Ltd
4th Floor, Capital Tower 1, MG Road,
Gurugram 122 002, Haryana, India

Penguin
Random House
India

First published in Penguin Books by Penguin Random House India and
Blue Salt Media 2017

ISBN 9780143427780

Typeset in Sabon by Manipal Digital Systems, Manipal

Printed at Repro India Limited

www.penguin.co.in

MIX
Paper from
responsible sources
FSC® C047271

To my mother, Chitra, and my brother, Prasad,
who mean the world to me

Contents

Foreword

While the Mumbai dons have blown their chances at redemption, their counterparts in Bengaluru have attained salvation. A little sleight of hand, some portfolio diversification, some personal transformation and, lo and behold, they emerged whitewashed, not necessarily of their sins, but of their dark shadows.

Unlike the Mumbai boys, the gangsters of Bengaluru think smartly. Although M.P. Jayaraj was eventually slain by another gangster, Muthappa Rai, he did start a tabloid called *Garibi Hatavo* and directly trained his guns at the government. The state simply picked him up and threw him in the slammer. While it is not known whether Muthappa Rai, Bengaluru's most feared don with a record of four known murders and a dozen other cases, has exorcised his past, but he has definitely moved ahead in the right direction to make his present legitimate. Ironically, Muthappa Rai has set up NGOs to salve his conscience even while plunging deep into the construction business. Impressed with his transformation, Bollywood is immortalizing him on celluloid.

Agni Sreedhar, another history-sheeter, has turned an author and a media baron. He is also dabbling in films and has even launched an apolitical outfit called Karunada Sene.

In comparison, the dons of Mumbai invariably came a cropper when they directly tried to associate themselves with Bollywood. Remember the washout of *Chori Chori Chupke Chupke*? While Chhota Rajan's *Vaastav* did well at the box office, it too got tainted by the producer. *Daddy*, a biopic on gangster-turned-politician Arun Gawli, also floundered at the box office.

In sharp contrast, the bad boys of Bengaluru proved that they were no bozos. The near fatal attack on Chhota Rajan in Bangkok could not have been executed successfully had it not been plotted by the *bhais* of Bengaluru. Dawood Ibrahim's financial empire, including his match fixing and betting rackets and real estate deals, was controlled by a Kannadiga: Sharad Shetty. Dawood Ibrahim's friend-turned-foe, Chhota Rajan wanted to cut his financial jugular and did the unthinkable—he got Sharad Shetty killed in Dubai, in a land where such crimes are deterred only by executions.

After Sharad Shetty, tired of their antics, Dubai deported the dons. Muthappa Rai was brought back to Bengaluru. But in the past fourteen years since his return, he has charted a new course.

Over the years, while writing on the Mumbai underworld, I stayed informed about the workings of the mafias in the other cities of India. However, I never got around to writing about them as I had no time for research. But I wanted these stories to be told and when I met Jyoti Shelar at *Mumbai Mirror*, where I was helming a bunch of reporters in 2016, I was impressed by her perseverance. I tasked her with chronicling the Bengaluru mafia. She made umpteen trips to the city and met all kinds of dubious characters but never gave up. She got an audience with Muthappa Rai, who even shared details of his personal life with her.

Throughout her legwork and research, I remained anxious about her and suffered pangs of extreme worry whenever she failed to give me the all-is-well update at night after she reached home. She got an earful whenever she missed the mandatory I-am-safe-and-have-returned calls.

I feel immense delight and pride in presenting this book to crime aficionados. And I am overjoyed at introducing my future rival and competitor in chronicling the mafia.

Jyoti Shelar, take a bow. Attagirl!

20 September 2017   S. Hussain Zaidi

Prologue

17 December 2016
Mekhri Circle, Bengaluru Palace Grounds

A patrol van stood next to the lavishly decorated gate of Tripura Vasini on Bengaluru's Palace Grounds. The much sought-after venue had hosted many a wedding, anniversary and birthday of Bengaluru's elite and influential. The decked-up gate, however, wasn't a patch on the grand affair that was taking place inside. A 500-metre red mud path led through the main gate to a parking lot where luxury wheels such as Bentleys, Mercedes and Audis were jostling for space. A dozen armed guards were manning the second entrance—a fairy tale pathway lit up with tiny bulbs leading to three metal detector gates. A prominent sign dangling above the gates read: 'Photography prohibited, videography prohibited, arms & ammunition not allowed.'

Beyond the checkpoints, the dapper host of the grand event was seen welcoming guests. Dressed in a dark-blue velvet blazer, 'reformed gangster' Muthappa Rai had a calm demeanour and could pass for a seasoned actor. The event was the last in a week-long series of wedding festivities for Rai's younger son Ricky, who had got married to his girlfriend Ketaki Kumar. A surprised Rai greeted me with a broad smile. 'From Mumbai, you have come here also?' he said, shaking hands with me.

The wedding reception was going to be held at Ela Estates in Yelahanka, a massive farm spread over 250 acres. It belonged to a close friend of Rai's. Unfortunately, untimely rainfall caused by Cyclone Vardah in the neighbouring state of Tamil Nadu had made the farm unsuitable for the high-heeled guests. So, at the eleventh hour, Rai deployed all his resources to make alternative arrangements at Tripura Vasini. An elegant 'change of venue' invitation card was designed, retaining the original theme of white-and-gold and was dispatched to all the guests, with the following words printed on them:

> Due to Vardah's Cyclonic effect, we have decided to change the venue of the wedding reception of Chi. Ricky Rai & Sou. Ketaki Kumar scheduled on Saturday, 17th December 2016 from ELA Estates, Muddanahalli, Yelahanka, Bengaluru–560064 to Tripura Vasini, Gate no 2, Bengaluru Palace Grounds, Mekhri Circle, Bengaluru–80. We deeply regret any inconvenience caused. Kindly note the change and oblige.

An insider estimate revealed that Rai spent over Rs 10 crore on the glitter and the glory surrounding his son's wedding. The highlight of the final event was a huge clear balloon that stood next to the entrance. Ensconced within the giant bubble was a flautist in a red gown playing an upbeat note. This curious exhibition of human talent and design drew many guests, who stopped by to admire the act, which was no less than a rare artefact on display at a museum. Some clicked pictures, bewildered and amused, while others waved at the flautist, receiving little more than a smile from her. At a corner, not very far from this quirky attraction, a three-member band of elegantly dressed women were performing a live act on a small stage decorated with white roses. Liquor flowed generously, with two bars serving the guests the best single malts, whisky, scotch and wines from around the world. For teetotallers, the drinks menu comprised mandarin mojito, nojito, ginger crush, exotica, thunder and lychee cooler. The food counter, spread across two sides to avoid overcrowding, was exhaustive. From Italian staples such as pizzas and pastas to Mangalorean classics such as chicken ghee roast and neer dosas, it was evident that Rai had left no stone unturned to ensure that his guests were well-fed.

The main stage for the newly-weds was decorated with white and pink flowers. The bride dazzled in a golden-sequined gown, while the groom was wearing a striped suit. The couple stood on the stage as the guests waited in a serpentine queue to get a chance to offer their blessings. Six drone cameras, which were hovering over the venue intermittently, would every now and then dive down and whiz over the heads of the guests, resulting in momentary exclamations of surprise and ruffled-up hairdos. And for those who couldn't access the stage, four large screens telecasted the proceedings live. This ensured that all the guests got a close look at every celebrity who had graced the occasion. Some of the notable attendees from among the 2000-odd guests included former Karnataka chief minister B.S. Yeddyurappa, sons of superstar Rajkumar—Puneeth Rajkumar and Shiva Rajkumar—actor Ganesh Bal, actor Yash and actress Radhika who is married to former Karnataka chief minister H.D. Kumaraswamy. Besides politicians and film personalities, many senior officers who had served in the Karnataka police force and handled criminal cases involving Rai also attended the event, posing for selfies with the ex-don.

There was no doubt that Rai had a fan following beyond average. All the guests strived for his attention and requested to be photographed with him. And he happily obliged them. Throughout the event, he shuttled back and forth between the stage and the seating area, posing for pictures and greeting people he hadn't earlier. When he spotted me for the second time, he enquired if I was impressed. '*Kaisa laga humara arrangement*? (Did you like our arrangement?)'

Rai skittered about the venue accompanied by two bodyguards. Dressed in black suits and holding sleek suitcases, the bodyguards resembled extras from the Hollywood blockbuster *Men in Black*, sans the dark glasses. It seemed they were ready to handle any unforeseen cash hurdle by instantly reaching inside their metallic attachés—an action they performed spontaneously.

For those oblivious to his legendary past, Rai could pass for an affluent businessman with expensive tastes and the wedding reception seemed like an affair he often hosted. That he had reigned over Bengaluru's underworld for over two decades wasn't something that met the eye. Now 'reformed' and acquitted in twelve criminal cases, including four murder charges and following twenty-two months in prison (the duration of his trial), Rai is breaking good. He has decided to give back to society and has carved himself as an influential social activist-cum-entrepreneur, whose deeds have earned him a huge following.

A gynaecologist, who was one of the guests, insisted, 'He is such a good man. He feels for the needy. He helps anyone and everyone who knocks on his doors. His past is gone. Today, there is no man with a heart like his.'

It was little over a month after Prime Minister Narendra Modi demonetized Rs 500 and Rs 1000 notes. The country's economy reacted nearly catastrophically. Weddings were called off and receptions postponed as the economy suddenly suffered a massive hit. Karnataka was in the news after former minister G. Janardhana Reddy hosted a lavish wedding of his daughter, Brahmani, in a meticulously constructed set depicting the great Vijayanagara empire, including the Lotus Mahal, palace of Krishnadevaraya, the great emperor of Vijayanagara, and a Vijaya Vittala temple. The grand affair pegged at a whopping Rs 100 crore was hosted at the same venue where Rai was hosting his son's wedding reception. As Indians reeled under a cash crunch, Reddy's obscene show of wealth turned into a Marie Antoinette moment. Questions were raised, social media trolled him extensively and Income Tax sleuths eventually conducted hasty surveys of the extravagant event.

Though not as flashy as the Reddy wedding, Rai's event was no less extravagant. But this time no questions were asked. After all the event was being hosted by someone who was once India's most wanted man, but now enjoyed the reputation of being Bengaluru's godfather.

The festivities went on till early morning and Rai made sure that he greeted every attendee before exiting the venue in his black Land Cruiser. Soon after he left, murmurs filled the air. High on spirits, some of Rai's followers bragged about the unparalleled access they had to the man while others kept mum as if they were secretly commissioned to snoop around for possible moles among the guests. A piece of gossip that was doing the rounds featured India's most wanted don Dawood Ibrahim's younger brother, Iqbal Kaskar. Apparently, Kaskar had expressed his interest to meet Rai at the reception to offer his greetings but the latter had politely refused to host him. Rumour mills added that Rai had offered to host a grand dinner for the don's brother in Bengaluru or Mumbai to make up for his refusal.

As one of the guests said, 'The man who played with guns all his life ensured that his past didn't catch up with his future.'

1

Birth of Bengaluru

The adventurous Kempe Gowda founded Bengaluru on a piece of land he believed was *gandu bhumi* (heroic land), after witnessing a tiny hare chasing a dog during one of his hunting expeditions. An ancestor of Yelahankanadu Prabhus dynasty, Kempe Gowda, decided to erect a mud fort in 1537 where stood a hamlet called Hale Bengaluru. Kempe Gowda envisioned a township within the fort, with meticulously planned streets, shops, temples, *pete* (market centres) and residential areas. Hale Bengaluru or Old Bengaluru eventually lent its name to Kempe Gowda's dream town.

There are many delightful stories behind the name. According to one legend, the great Hoysala king Veera Ballala Raya was once returning from a hunting trip, exhausted and hungry. He requested an old woman for something to eat, and in turn, she offered him boiled beans, the only leftover food she had in her kitchen.

Touched by her hospitality and generosity, Ballala Raya named the hamlet Benda Kalooru or the 'town of boiled beans'. The name gradually morphed to Bengaluru and then further colloquialized to Bangalore. In 2005, Jnanpith-awardee U.R. Ananthamurthy proposed that Bangalore be officially renamed Bengaluru, a suggestion duly accepted by the Karnataka government in 2014.

In the nineteenth century, the British established their cantonment in Bengaluru. Kempe Gowda's mud fort was gradually demolished in parts to accommodate the expanding township within. The cantonment and the old city were later merged, forming the base of the vast city that Bengaluru would come to be in the following years.

The influx of people and the city's growing popularity is eloquently described by M. Fazlul Hassan in his book *Bangalore Through the Centuries*:

> Bangalore's salubrious climate, which is compared to that of Nice of France on the shore of the Mediterranean, drew a large number of settlers. Hither came armymen, pensioners, homesteaders, and people of all walks of life. Hither also came girls, not deficient in glamour, from good old 'Blighty' (England) seeking matrimonial prospects amongst the white settlers and army officers. English life became the fashion of the day. Ballroom dances enlivened the nights in the wake of orchestra filling the air. At the nightclubs, jovial men excelled in glacial wit while vivacious beauties baited attention with swaying charms. At times, however, night entertainment was highly spiced when Bangalore's bohemia preferred

after-theatre-hours restaurants where they could sup at ease and drink rum, gin, sherry and all that, but in the end some of them somehow got into a mess! Brigade Road at that time contained many bars, taverns and public houses like Adelphi Shades, Elysium, New Inn, etc.—where attractive women often waited at the tables for chance company.

By this time, Bengaluru had earned the reputation of a 'Garden City'. Besides the two large gardens that the city boasted of—Lal Bagh, a pleasure garden made by Haider Ali and Tipu Sultan in the eighteenth century, and Cubbon Park, created by a British chief engineer—there were ten other expansive parks and over eighty small gardens that added to its lush green cover. Some called it 'Pensioners's Paradise', others 'AC City' or 'Air-Conditioned City' way before it came to be known as the 'Silicon Valley of India' and the 'Information Technology (IT) Capital of India'.

In the early 1950s, the central government launched several public sector units in Bengaluru—Bharat Electronics Limited, Hindustan Machine Tools Limited, Indian Telephone Industries Limited, Hindustan Aeronautics Limited (HAL) and Bharat Earth Movers Limited, etc.—before the private sector made an entry with companies such as Motor Industries Company Limited (MICO). MICO employed over one lakh workers, mostly migrants, in its initial years. These new units functioned seamlessly alongside Bengaluru's many mills: Maharaja Mill, Minerva Mill, Ramkumar Mill, among others. The working class thus made inroads into the city, sowing seeds of labour unions. The affluent and the sophisticated chose to settle in extensions such as Malleshwaram and Basavanagudi while the labour class flocked towards the expanding slums in Srirampura, Neelasandra, Tannery Road, Yeshwanthpur and Shivajinagar. This period saw an influx of Tamil migrants into the city.

During those days, every locality had at least one tough, well-built man who commanded respect and fear. Clashes were rare as these men laid down their jurisdictions and established a mutual understanding. Malleshwaram had Market Jaggi, a vegetable vendor who wielded great authority over the marketplace and the vendors. Besides managing his own business, he would settle disputes among vendors, dictate pricing and resolve issues related to market dealings. In return for his services, he demanded a small sum from each vendor. Kalasipalya had Ganapathy, Srirampura had Miyan Pehelwan and Shivajinagar had its *pehelwans*. Their work involved settling business disputes, resolving family problems and collecting donations to organize religious events such as Ganesh Utsav and Annamma Devi Mahotsav. And all this while holding themselves in high regard.

At that time, there were limited avenues to collect *mamool*, a Kannada term for extortion money. These men would flex their muscles at the brothels and hooch dens that churned out low-quality alcohol.

Bengaluru was then famous for *andar bahar* or *katti*, an illegal gambling card game. In narrow alleys, groups of men would gather to bet on a card picked out from a deck. The man conducting the game would deal one card at a time—face down or 'inside' (andar) and one face up or 'outside' (bahar)—till a match to the original card appeared. Whoever got the card that matched with the original won the game and the money. Besides small bets by roadside gamblers, andar bahar was a big hit in gambling dens where slightly bigger amounts were at stake. The local strongmen soon got wind of this fledgling business and began targeting them for mamool. Even a meagre collection of Rs 5 a day would keep them happy. The only thing that mattered to them was the larger-than-life persona that they enjoyed in their localities. Till then, there was no trace of what Kannadigas call *bhugataloka* or the underworld. The city was still unfamiliar to organized crime or notorious criminals.

The small crimes that made it to the newspapers were mostly about the busting of illicit liquor dens, arrests of arrack sellers or conmen and their activities. The *Deccan Herald* on 3 June 1955 reported in an article headlined 'Prohibition Cases', that twelve people were arrested and nineteen pots, one bottle of fermented wash and eighty-five drams of illicitly distilled (ID) liquor were seized in a raid.

In another *Deccan Herald* article on 5 March 1965 headlined '2 con men caught, taken to police', it was reported how an alert taxi driver had foiled an attempt by two tricksters to get away with the jewellery of an old woman. According to the report, Narayanaswamy (68) and Ramaiah (45) won the confidence of an old man in Frazer Town. The duo had approached the old man on the pretext of finalizing a 'deal' about a house. One day, when the old man was not at home, Narayanaswamy and Ramaiah went there and engaged his wife, Rathnammal, in a conversation. A little later, the men complimented Rathnammal on her jewellery and expressed the desire to get similar pieces made for their wives. Rathnammal took off her jewellery and gave it to the men so they could get a closer look at the designs. But the minute she left them alone, the men slipped out of the house and made a dash for a taxi that could have helped them escape. Rathnammal on second thoughts smelt a rat and ran outside. She yelled at them to come back but the men ignored her calls and started walking briskly towards the taxi. The driver, realizing the situation, refused to start the car. The people of the locality then nabbed the conmen and handed them over to the Frazer Town police.

These were also the initial years when Tamil activists had begun carrying out anti-Hindi protests. Several of these marches often turned violent. This was also the time when Kannadigas woke up to the growing Tamil presence in the city, which then marked the beginning of anti-Tamil protests led by the Kannadigas. Bengaluru had become a hub of Tamilians; this inadvertently led to the language of the land, Kannada, losing ground. If one walked down the commercial areas of Bengaluru early in the morning, one would spot large groups of people reading Tamil newspapers.

Around the same time, in 1956, Kannada-speaking regions were brought under a single state, Mysore. The name was later changed to Karnataka in the year 1973.

Eminent writer Prathibha Nandakumar in her article for *Bangalore Mirror* had once written:

> The Republic states were formulated based on language and the greater Karnataka came into being. However, not much was done with regard to Kannada and following an advertisement in a newspaper calling invitations from 'painters for Bangalore municipality, knowledge of Tamil and Telugu compulsory' writer A.N. Krishna Rao and his band of faithful followers launched a Kannada movement.

Bengaluru remained at the centre of the Kannada movement. Writer M. Ramamurthy, who is credited for the yellow- and red-striped Kannada flag, and A.N. Krishna Rao went on to deliver many speeches advocating a pro-Kannada language and culture. They also petitioned that all cinema hall owners who played only non-Kannada films during the 1960s give preference to Kannada films.

Another activist who took centre stage during the Kannada movement was Vatal Nagaraj. Though known as a great orator, Nagaraj and his supporters resorted to violent protests. In the 1960s, he and his supporters reportedly burnt down a cinema hall for playing a Tamil movie. Nagaraj also led a protest against a British war memorial rock opposite the city's municipality offices, eventually forcing the government to bring it down. The municipality is now known as the Bruhat

Bengaluru Mahanagara Palike (BBMP) and a statue of Kempe Gowda stands in place of the war memorial at Narasimharaja Square.

In her essay titled 'Battles for Bengaluru: Reterritorialising the City', published by the Centre for the Study of Culture and Society, Bengaluru, writer Janaki Nair narrates the events evocatively:

> Kannada activists were not slow in seeking an end to Hindi domination, but also a reduced Tamil presence, demanding films in their own language. The link between linguistic and cultural dominance was most visible in the realm of cinema, since the Tamil film held its own against Hollywood and Hindi films in the city. Kannada films were a distant fourth or even fifth in this hierarchy. Controversy first broke out over *Kanchi Thalaivan* (1963), which portrayed the Pallava kings' triumph over the Chalukyas. The same groups, led by Vatal Nagaraj's Kannada Chaluvaligars, which had staged their protest against the cenotaph, threatened the closure of theatres where Tamil films were being shown.

While there were these activists on the one hand, there was a group of disgruntled young men, on the other hand, which contributed to the Kannada movement in its own way. These were the die-hard fans of Karnataka's matinee idol and demigod Rajkumar. By demanding that theatres screen Rajkumar movies, his fan club gave the issue of Kannada prominence a unique spin. While the superstar himself lived in Madras (present-day Chennai), his fans in Bengaluru took to the streets to tear and blacken posters of Tamil movies, ransack theatres, shout slogans and demand that Kannada movies top the list. Their grouse was that all major theatres like State in Gandhi Nagar, Kino on SC Road, Lakshmi in Balaji Nagar, Ajanta in Ulsoor, Lavanya on St John's Road and Geeta, which was in the heart of the city, in Kempegowda Circle, played Tamil movies. The remaining few would play Hindi films. It was difficult to find one theatre playing a Kannada movie in a Kannada state. On rare days when a Rajkumar film was screened, fans went berserk, taking to the streets in large numbers. This passionate reaction kept the police on their toes all the time.

Thus, the Kannada movement gave rise to hooliganism in Bengaluru but the cause was a noble one: to give Kannada its due recognition. However, as the city began changing its dynamics, so did the causes of crimes.

2

From Pehelwans to Bhugataloka

Loud cheers and claps filled a small room in Kodigehalli, a suburb of Bengaluru. A six-foot-tall man, covered in soft red soil, slapped his thighs and arms seconds before grabbing his opponent's neck. The opponent struggled to free himself. Taking advantage of the moment, Mune Gowda wrapped his legs around his challenger's and pinned him down.

Another round of applause filled the room, which reeked of a concoction of ghee, kumkum, haldi and saffron, ingredients mixed with the red soil before the wrestlers started fighting. On one wall of the room, a hook held in place Mune Gowda's shirts and trousers while on the opposite wall was a garlanded photo of Lord Hanuman, a Hindu deity revered for his strength and courage.

Mune Gowda slapped his thighs and arms once again, gesturing another wrestler who stood in line to take him on. This match too lasted barely two minutes before Mune Gowda overpowered his opponent and pinned him down. He then gestured the group of ten spectators to leave. Such was his authority that no one dared to stay even for an extra second. It was time for him to pump muscles and head for a bath. This ritual was always followed by him gulping down two litres of milk and munching on a fistful of almonds. The milk came from a cowshed near the *garadi mane* or *kushti* (wrestling) house where Mune Gowda practised and the almonds came from a grocery store next door, both complimentary. Mune Gowda also gorged on *ragimudde*, a nutritious recipe of finger millet flour popular among bodybuilders of those days and a staple in parts of Karnataka.

Belonging to the Vokkaliga community that Kempe Gowda also belonged to, Mune Gowda had taken to *nada* kushti, the traditional Indian form of wrestling, since he was ten years old. Pehelwans like Mune Gowda stuck to the ancient sport and used it to their benefit. His mere presence in a room was enough to intimidate the people. In a way, his muscle power and brashness made him Bengaluru's first powerful rowdy. There were other local extortionists but Mune Gowda's aggressiveness and ability to defeat his opponents put him in a different league.

But Mune Gowda never killed anyone. The only time his name appeared in the police files was when he went about collecting mamool and was refused. He crushed any defiance with violent physical assault. He would stand at the doors of small-time arrack sellers and brothels and the owners would come out and hand over the money, without Mune Gowda uttering even a single word. He also targeted moneylenders, mostly from the Marwari community, to create an image of a do-gooder, as Marwaris were notorious for extracting huge interests and paying measly sums in return for mortgaged land and jewellery. Interestingly, Mune Gowda never enjoyed any of this money himself. He was the son of a wealthy landlord. It was the power that he revelled in.

Legend has it that Mune Gowda's brashness grew so much that the locals decided to teach him a lesson. They formed a group of half a dozen young, well-built men to attack him. But when the gang eventually faced him, armed with big shiny swords, they could not dare to attack him. Only one of them managed to land a strike that cost Mune Gowda three fingers of his right hand. But it could barely scare him to quit his ways. He continued to rule and crush his opponents. He even managed to regularly ride a two-wheeler despite having only a thumb and the ring finger on one hand.

Mune Gowda was a serial womanizer who sought a new attachment every other week. Attracted to his daring personality, many women would give in to his passes. His rivals decided to use Mune Gowda's roving eye to his disadvantage. He would often spend time at Kapali Bar near Kapali Talkies. The owner of Kapali Talkies, Rajgopal, had hired Mune Gowda as his bodyguard. A trade union leader, he had first sought support from Mune Gowda for a labour union issue at Bharat Electronics Limited. Impressed by his command over people, Rajgopal hired him at Kapali Talkies to manage unlawful elements and handle actor Rajkumar's unruly fans. Every evening after work, Mune Gowda would gulp down peg after peg at Kapali Bar, ogling at women, whistling and passing lewd remarks. One evening his passes were not met with smirks or profanities as a young attractive woman smiled back at him. Mune Gowda took it as an invitation and stumbled out of the bar following her. A few days later, Mune Gowda rented a house for the woman and started visiting her every day. One of his punters told him that he was suspicious of the woman. But Mune Gowda was blinded by lust.

One day, Mune Gowda went out for a movie with his new girlfriend. Throughout the screening, the woman kept going out of the theatre several times, but Mune Gowda did not suspect anything. After the movie, when the two walked out of the theatre, fifteen people attacked him. He fought hard and drove everyone away. His girlfriend too had disappeared.

After this failed plan, Mune Gowda's rivals hooked him up with another woman. Once again, Mune Gowda rented a house for his new girlfriend and started living with her. This time, however, the attackers had a more brutal scheme in mind. The woman fed Mune Gowda crushed glass mixed with his food after which he landed in hospital and took a long time to recover. By the time he was discharged, his health had deteriorated considerably. The pehelwan could not take the sudden loss of power and eventually died after a severe anxiety attack. However, this wasn't the end of hooliganism in Bengaluru. It was just the beginning. Kodigehalli's Mune

Gowda had inspired many budding pehelwans to take up his mantle.

The wrestling culture of Bengaluru dates back to the time of Kempe Gowda, who was an avid wrestler himself. It was then adopted by the monarchs who ruled the state of Mysore that later became Karnataka. The royals held grand competitions of *malla-yuddha* during the festival of Dussehra. The winners of these competitions were no less popular than film stars.

During the 1950s and the 1960s, Bengaluru had more than 150 garadi manes, mostly in areas like Shivajinagar, Cubbonpete, Cottonpete, Balepete and Chikpete. Even as the Britishers introduced sports like golf, polo and cricket, Bengalureans remained loyal to kushti, a sport that played a vital role in their fight for independence. During the freedom struggle, women in Bengaluru would spill ragi on the road when British officers and sepoys toured on their horses. As soon as the horses stepped on the ragi, they would slip, throwing off the riders. Pehelwans would then pounce on the men and overpower them with the help of other locals.

New entrants in the garadi manes had to pay Re 1 as admission fee. The monthly fee was *entanni* or 50 paise. Entering a garadi was more like enrolling oneself into a life of discipline. It was therefore termed *sadhane*, a spiritual rigour to achieve something. On the very first day, the new entrant would have to carry turmeric, kumkum, a piece of cloth called *langot*, twelve bananas, two coconuts, tulsi leaves, flowers, four lemons, a betel leaf, areca nut, camphor, incense sticks, castor oil and half a kilogram of sweets. An elaborate ritual was then carried out by the senior coach before the newcomer was allowed to enter the mud pit. The garadis were built in a peculiar manner. One entered through a door not more than four feet in height into a room with huge paintings of Lord Hanuman and other Hindu gods hanging on the walls. The height of the door was deliberately kept low. The wrestlers would have to bend down while entering—a symbolic gesture of paying their respects to Lord Hanuman and to the garadi. Women were banned from entering the garadi for two reasons: Lord Hanuman was a *brahmachari* (devout bachelor), and they could distract the wrestlers.

The tough discipline wearied away to a certain extent when some pehelwans began using their muscle power to gain recognition. In desperation to show their dominance, they became self-proclaimed 'saviours'.

In the 1950s, one such pehelwan was Yathiraj from Cubbonpete. He practised at the Bachegowda Garadi, which dates back to 1907. It was later renamed Sri Kodandarama Vyayamashala. Yathiraj began attacking men who misbehaved with women, intervened in cases of domestic violence, caught thieves and bashed them with his bare hands.

Veteran garadi pehelwan R. Shanmugam remembers Yathiraj as a man who stood for justice. 'He took up social causes. He was the dada of the area,' says Shanmugam, who has been living in Cubbonpete since his birth in 1935.

A senior of Yathiraj, revered pehelwan N. Nanjannappa had rightly predicted that competitions and a show of muscle strength would eventually lead pehelwans away from sadhane. Nanjannappa, who worked in a government-run printing press, insisted that the pehelwans should only concentrate on exercising and not indulge in any other activity. 'Otherwise they would be provoked by rowdyism,' he had predicted. Nanjannappa's words lost importance over the years.

Towards the end of the 1950s, Bengaluru's garadi manes supported the Hindu right-wing political party Jana Sangh. In areas like Cubbonpete, which was dominated by the *devangas* or a community of weavers, the tilt was prominently towards Hinduism. They focused on Sangh activities of singing bhajans, celebrating Hindu festivals with grandeur and organizing other religious and cultural events to emphasize the presence of Hindus in the area. The pehelwans were also used by small-time political leaders to spread fear. Miyan Pehelwan from Srirampura worked as a porter at a railway station and wrestled at a garadi mane in his free time. He became extremely notorious in the 1960s for accepting contracts to attack people. Miyan Pehelwan was among the first antisocial pehelwans to form a small gang of 'supari attackers'. After him came Mune Gowda, and others like Chudi Pehelwan and Gugga Pehelwan from Shivajinagar, who began exploiting innocent people by their show of strength.

Mamool had become a regular source of income for the pehelwans now. All they had to do was stand outside brothels or gambling clubs and glare at the owners. Within minutes, they would have bundles of cash thrust into their palms. When their demands were not met, they would beat up the owner and the staff, which was enough to keep them going for months. The news of the bashing would spread like wildfire. The mamool collection would go up once again and continue smoothly till someone else dared to put his foot down only to get roughed up.

It is from Bengaluru's once-revered wrestling houses that the city got its most dangerous and notorious don. He came into the limelight in the 1970s and became the first pehelwan to make it big in bhugataloka.

3

Indira Brigade

Prime Minister Indira Gandhi on 25 June 1975 imposed a state of Emergency in the country, suspending fundamental rights and creating a deep sense of anti-incumbency. Civil liberties were curbed, media was censored, gatherings and rallies were prohibited and her opponents were thrown into jail. She maintained that the Emergency was the need of the hour and required for the betterment of the people. But her opponents simmered with anger and joined hands to form a strong coalition to bring her down. As many as thirteen opposition parties came together to form the Janata Party, which swept into power in the 1977 Union elections, forcing Indira Gandhi to step down. Consequently, Morarji Desai became the first non-Congress prime minister of India.

While the Janata Party came into power in the majority of states, the Congress managed to maintain its hold on Karnataka. Then chief minister of Karnataka,

D. Devaraj Urs was a staunch follower of Indira Gandhi, her right-hand man and confidant. Urs belonged to the Arasu community of the Mysore royals. But the dominant castes in Karnataka's political and economic circles were the Lingayats and the Vokkaligas. Such was their hold that barring one, all chief ministers before Urs had been from either of these two castes. The state's first elected chief minister was Kengal Hanumanthaiah, a Vokkaliga. After him, another Vokkaliga, Kadidal Manjappa, took over. Post the unification of Karnataka, four powerful Congress leaders from the Lingayat community became chief ministers—Siddavanahalli Nijalingappa, Basappa Danappa Jatti, S.R. Kanthi and Veerendra Patil.

In 1972, the caste barrier broke when Urs was appointed the chief minister despite several powerful and promising Lingayat Congress leaders being in line. Urs neither had the money nor the caste card. All he had was the support of Indira Gandhi, who was then at the pinnacle of her political career having crushed her opponents in the 1971 Union elections. The tagline 'garibi hatao, desh bachao' (eradicate poverty, save the country), coined by her, had become immensely popular. Urs too rode on the wave of her success.

The anti-Indira Gandhi movement post the Emergency started making Urs restless. He knew that his mere closeness with Indira Gandhi was not enough to run the state and command the respect of his ministers and people. He could feel the mounting pressure from Lingayat leaders of north Karnataka and the Vokkaliga leaders from the south, both of whom were aggressively trying to dominate over him on the political front. He began to realize that his proximity with Indira Gandhi was inconsequential outside New Delhi, the seat of the Congress high command. Sensing it was time to re-strategize his political game, Urs began to work on three fronts. He started building his political, financial and muscle power.

His first move was to mobilize the backward communities and gather a significant number of supporters. To face the dominant Lingayats and the Vokkaligas, he sought the support of the other backward communities in the state such as the Kurubas (shepherds), the Edigas (toddy tappers) and the Ganigas (oil pressers). Even minorities such as the Kshatriya Marathas and the Muslims were pulled on board. Soon he was looked upon as the man who was sympathetic towards the downtrodden, which strengthened his political image. His increasing political clout also gave rise to an urgent need for a bigger cash coffer. Urs sought the support of liquor baron and industrialist Hari Khoday and his likes for financial power. But the much-needed muscle power at this point came from his son-in-law M.D. Nataraj.

Urs, who hailed from Hunsur Taluka in Mysuru, was married early to 11-year-old Chikkammanni. The couple had three daughters, Chandraprabha, Nagarathnammanni and Bharathi. While studying at Maharani College, Nagarathnammanni, who was lovingly called Nagarathna, fell in love with M.D. Nataraj, a medical student. Nataraj belonged to the Kuruba caste.

The dramatic turn of political events had led Urs to completely ignore his family. He was oblivious to the fact that Nagarathna had secretly married Nataraj. A fuming Urs used all the resources at his disposal to scoop out every detail about Nataraj's life and family. His men came back with unpleasant information. Nataraj, as it turned out, was not the man whom Urs would have liked his daughter to marry. He was popular among women and led a life that was deemed inappropriate for the family member of a chief minister. Some also alleged that Nagarathna was not his first wife. After much persuasion by Nagarathna, Urs accepted the alliance and married off the couple in a grand ceremony. He even bought a house for them in Malleshwaram. Even though Urs wanted Nataraj to complete his degree and settle abroad with his daughter, he made him a Member of the Legislative Council (MLC) upon the latter's insistence. Nataraj had strong political ambitions and did not want to settle abroad.

By accepting Nataraj, political pundits believe that Urs played a masterstroke. He not only gained unconditional support of the Kurubas, but also won a political upper hand by accepting a man from a backward class as his son-in-law. As time passed, they grew closer and Urs started treating Nataraj like a son.

Soon Nataraj rose to become the most powerful man in the party under his father-in-law's leadership. The trust was mutual as Urs also relied on his advice for important decisions. At that time, R. Gundu Rao, who later went on to become Karnataka's chief minister, and

F.M. Khan were upcoming Youth Congress leaders. They were both close to Sanjay Gandhi, younger son of Indira Gandhi, and were said to be unhappy with Nataraj's wild-card entry into the Congress party. Nataraj was well aware of the resentment and the way he was looked at within the party. To counter the hostility, he went a step ahead and formed the 'Indira Brigade', something on the lines of the Youth Congress. Unofficially though, it was an unorganized group of muscular men who were overzealous Indira Gandhi supporters.

Nataraj, in a press statement, had once said that he wanted to model Indira Brigade on the lines of Komitet Gosudarstvennoy Bezopasnosti (KGB)—the main security agency of the erstwhile Soviet Union. Nataraj envisioned that his Indira Brigade would function like a powerful and robust intelligence unit. The main aim of the brigade was to protect Indira Gandhi. It is said that the formation of a brigade in her name had pleased the 'Iron Lady' immensely. She would inquire about the organization whenever she had visitors from Bengaluru in New Delhi.

Nataraj was looking for a strong man to lead the brigade. He found the ideal candidate while attending a Kannada Rajotsava event, celebrated on 1 November every year to commemorate the day of Unification of Karnataka. The man was M.P. Jayaraj, a pehelwan known for his rowdiness.

Nataraj had begun identifying himself as the brigadier and Jayaraj was inducted as second in command. The brigade, however, had no defined goals, organizational structure or even an office. It was more of an informal group of people, mainly rowdies, who took pride in being a part of something that had political approval. The members of the group did little constructive work and were often seen in gangs riding motorbikes, and creating menace for the locals. They went around flexing their muscles and boasting about their clout within the Congress party. Journalist R. Somanath, who has analysed the crime and politics of Bengaluru, described Indira Brigade as nothing but a group of local hooligans without an agenda. 'The rowdies got a political stamp for their activities. They simply gave a respectful name to it and called it Indira Brigade.'

Many influential politicians of today were a part of Indira Brigade back then. It helped in strengthening Urs's grip on Karnataka politics. He had finally found the muscle power that he had longed for. Due to lack of an organizational structure and clarity in terms of vision and ideology, Indira Brigade died an unceremonious death not too long after its inception. But it gave birth to a rowdy who, with strong political backing, shaped the organized crime world of Bengaluru.

4

Pioneers of Bhugataloka

M.P. Jayaraj

Fifteen-year-old Puttaswamappa was lured to Bengaluru sometime in 1925, all the way from Mysuru, a picturesque town in Karnataka. After doing odd jobs for several years, Mysore Puttaswamappa—as he called himself—joined HAL as a manual labourer. The six-foot-tall man had two obsessions, bodybuilding in the garadi and getting into fights to draw attention to himself. He knew that his job as a manual labourer would never bring him the fame he deeply craved for. So he started taking up people's issues, even fighting against those who exploited the poor, and made a name for himself. But his image as a messiah was tarnished when he opened a *matka* (gambling den) business.

Puttaswamappa, who belonged to the Ganiga community, married twice. He had three children, two boys and a girl, with his first wife Thayamma. The eldest son, M.P. Mahadev, went on to become a national-level football player. His younger son, M.P. Jayadev, followed in his father's footsteps and joined HAL. His daughter was married off at a young age. Thayamma, however, died when her children were very young. Puttaswamappa then married Thayamma's younger sister, Puttathayamma. The couple had seven children. In 1948, Puttathayamma gave birth to her first son, Jayaraj, named after the lord of victory. He came to be known as Mysore Puttaswamappa Jayaraj: M.P. Jayaraj.

Puttaswamappa and his large family lived in a massive house at Siddhapura village. Their house was surrounded by a guava farm and huge rocks. Jayaraj went to a Kannada medium school, United Mission, and dropped out after Class VII. While he was growing up, Jayaraj closely observed his father and copied his mannerisms. Like his father, he too spent long hours in the garadi. He spoke in a stern voice and constantly craved for fame and attention. Jayaraj too joined HAL in 1968. Like his father, he stood up against injustice and gradually veered into the *kala dhandas* (shady businesses). As a young boy, he often saw policemen harassing his father and those memories stayed with him. For him, the policemen were *nayi* (dogs).

Puttaswamappa saw a lot of himself in Jayaraj. He knew that the boy would do well for himself and the family. One day, when Jayaraj returned home, he saw his father being roughed up by the police. After they left, he ran up to his father and asked what had led to the assault. His father said: 'The police are inhuman bastards who only harass innocent people.' What he had held back from Jayaraj was that only a few weeks ago he had dragged the sub-inspector of Ashok Nagar Police Station on the road and kicked him in public. The inspector had incurred Puttaswamappa's wrath by raiding his matka den. The policeman, however, did not register any complaint fearing that the matka boss wouldn't let him off the second time.

Puttaswamappa was unmoved by the incident. He put his arm around Jayaraj's shoulder and told him something that Jayaraj valued till the very end.

'*Yarigu bhaya padabaaradhu, bhaya pattare avaru nammannu bhaya padisutthare.* (Don't fear anyone. If you fear, they will keep intimidating you.)'

Jayaraj's stint with HAL lasted only for two years. His younger sister Hemavati blames herself for Jayaraj's ouster from the company. 'He took a long leave to make arrangements for my wedding and when he returned to work, they fired him,' she says. But old Bengalureans believe there is a different story. What caused the exit was his first public display of disruptive behaviour.

In 1970, Jayaraj learnt of the unscrupulous moneylender Baddi Chinnappa, who ran a chit fund called Laxmi Finance near HAL. His clients were mainly labourers from HAL, whose transaction records Chinnappa maintained in pocket-sized books. He had over one hundred such books locked up in his office; the borrowers had no access to them. Since most of the people who borrowed money were uneducated,

Chinnappa would often manipulate the records by inflating the amounts he had given on credit. Unaware, the unsuspecting labourers would continue to repay the loans for a very long time, weighed down by huge interest.

One day, in true Bollywood potboiler style, Jayaraj barged into the office of Laxmi Finance, vandalized the place and attacked Chinnappa. He broke open the cupboard and took out all 150 passbooks and distributed them to the labourers. The act almost instantly made him a hero. Touched by his sense of justice, the poor labourers wept and fell at his feet. Jayaraj felt important and revered, something he had always craved for. His heroism rendered him jobless as HAL handed him the pink slip.

A few months later, Jayaraj, who was still living with Puttaswamappa, was woken up by sudden cries from outside the house.

'Anna, save us! Anna, save us!'

Jayaraj opened the door to find a massive crowd of people from the slum near Siddhapura Gate. Two truckloads of people had arrived to displace the slum dwellers at the behest of the city's development department. As the news of the demolition squad's arrival reached the slum dwellers, they rushed to seek Puttaswamappa's help. The patriarch pacified them but put Jayaraj in charge of the situation. Jayaraj picked up a long machete from behind the door and charged towards the demolition squad.

'If anybody dares to step out of the vehicle, I will chop him to death,' Jayaraj thundered, brandishing the machete. The demolition squad hurriedly left the spot making Jayaraj the hero for the second time.

Jayaraj's image as a messiah began to grow as more people approached him for instant justice. By then, he had also begun extorting money from brothel owners. Those who refused to pay him mamool were roughed up.

During those days, Wilson Garden was the border of Bengaluru. Near the border was a graveyard and a slum inhabited by a large number of Tamil migrants. A man named Baby ran a brothel and brewed country liquor in a *bhatti sarai* (hooch den). Jayaraj threatened Baby and ordered him to pay a monthly mamool. But Baby was not intimidated.

'You do whatever you can. I will not part with a single penny,' he challenged Jayaraj.

It did not take long for Jayaraj to come back with an answer. He returned with his cronies, a gang that he had formed and nurtured over the years. Kiki Raja, Patri Narayana, Paisa and Nagesha reached Baby's den, led by Jayaraj. The five-foot-eight gangster held Baby by his collar, lifted him off the ground and chopped off his ear with his signature machete. His gang vandalized the brothel and the hooch den and left Baby in a pool of blood. The following day Baby went to Jayaraj's house with a dozen of his gang members. Puttaswamappa opened the door to tell him Jayaraj was not at home. Although at first it seemed like Baby had come to avenge the attack but it later turned out that he was an emotional wreck after the previous day's encounter. Bandaged around the head, a teary-eyed Baby took out the severed ear from his pocket and started narrating his son's brutality to Puttaswamappa. But Puttaswamappa was unmoved. On the contrary, the sixty-three-year-old started beating up Baby and his accomplices before throwing them out of the house. He warned them never to return again. The news of Jayaraj's attack on Baby spread like wildfire. It sent a strong signal to all those who had dared to refuse him money.

Bengaluru used to have a lush green cover, replete with forests and hills. Kempe Gowda had constructed four towers in four corners of the city. One was erected near Palace Guttahalli that is now known as Sadashivanagar, another near Ulsoor Lake, the third one at Lalbagh and the fourth one near Basavanagudi. To date, these towers are protected monuments and their design is the emblem of BBMP.

These towers stood amid thick forests and were frequented by couples who wanted to steal some private moments with each other. Soon rowdies got wind of this. They often accosted the couples and looted them. Once when an Air Force officer drove to one of the towers with his fiancée, a group of rowdies held him at knifepoint and robbed him. The incident became sensational as the victim was a defence official. The police immediately sprang into action and arrested Ramchandra Rao, Blade Raja, Police Jaggi and Jayaraj. They made Modus Operandi Bureau (MOB) cards against all the four accused. The case, which was handled by the Vyalikaval police, ended in conviction. While the incident earned Jayaraj the nickname 'Robbery Jayaraj', it was Ramchandra Rao who came to be known as the 'Robbery King of Bengaluru'.

Despite everything, Jayaraj remained a small-time rowdy till Nataraj spotted him at a Kannada Rajotsava event. Nataraj was impressed not just by Jayaraj's following and clout, but also by his build. Jayaraj had strong muscles and a fit body that he kept toned by spending several hours at the Annaiyappa Garadi. A week after the Rajotsava, Nataraj offered Jayaraj a job that simply required him to shadow the former and be a part of Indira Brigade. Nataraj also introduced him to Urs. The lure of a strong political connection prompted Jayaraj to accept the offer. His eighty-two criminal cases in various police stations were no hindrance at all. The cases ranged from attempt to murder, extortion to robbery and dacoity. Jayaraj was now a wanted criminal in almost half the city's police stations.

His main source of income continued to be the mamool he collected from brothels and gambling dens. After joining Indira Brigade, his brand equity increased. Soon Jayaraj bought himself a white Ambassador, a premium luxury vehicle in those days. In order to keep the messiah image alive, he started a newspaper, *Garibi Hatavo*—a name inspired by Indira Gandhi's 1971 election tagline. Priced at 50 paise, the four-page weekly's tagline was: 'Boldest Kannada weekly from Bangalore'. The logo of the newspaper was that of a tiger, representative of the common man, pouncing on the babus and the rich. The symbolic victory of the poor over the rich made the paper an instant hit. For a newspaper to print 5000 copies in the 1970s was unheard of. Every week, as fresh copies were printed, young boys would pick up bundles and go around shouting the headlines near temples, railway and bus stations and outside government offices.

The newspaper had a straightforward agenda—it was pro-Congress, anti-Opposition and strongly anti-police. Each edition had a strongly worded editorial by Jayaraj on page two, where he mostly criticized the police. Needless to say, on most days it was Jayaraj who made the headlines in his own newspaper.

Jayaraj's *Garibi Hatavo* had a tabloid bent, where several sting operations were conducted on the police. The policemen would routinely be caught on camera taking bribes, lounging in brothels and consuming liquor. The police fraternity became the main readers of the paper. They would secretly purchase the paper and keep folded copies in their pockets and read them at home. Reading *Garibi Hatavo* served two purposes for them—to check if they had been featured in that day's edition and if any of their colleagues had been caught on camera doing something illegal.

Jayaraj did not care to make profits from the newspaper. There was no compulsion that the hawkers had to sell all the copies. On most days, the leftover copies would be distributed for free. What mattered to him was that his words were reaching the masses. Though Jayaraj was the editor, publisher and owner of the paper, he had hired a battery of ghostwriters to write the articles and convey his thoughts.

Jayaraj had donned the mantle of Robin Hood. He would extort from the rich and give to the poor. He sponsored weddings, naming ceremonies, and even gave money to those who could not afford to perform the last rites of their loved ones. Jayaraj's sister-in-law Nirmala, who was also his niece, observed him closely while she was growing up. 'What he did outside was beyond our comprehension. At home, he was the most loving person around. He would laugh, crack jokes and take us all for movies in the drive-in theatre. On the way back, we would stop for ice cream.' Nirmala fondly recalls how Jayaraj would hand over a Rs 100 note every time they met. 'It was big money for us in those days.' Jayaraj was married to a woman named Gayatri. However, the couple didn't have any children. It was said that he had a son with one of his mistresses, a fact his family was aware of.

With his increasing popularity, Jayaraj amassed friends and foes. One of them was Thigalarpete Gopi, another garadi pehelwan. Gopi extorted money from small-time businessmen, most of whom were Marwaris. Jayaraj crossed paths with Gopi when his gang demanded mamool from a shopkeeper who was already paying Gopi. The Marwari complained to Gopi, who felt threatened by Jayaraj's entry into his area. Wasting no time, Gopi took Jayaraj by complete surprise and attacked him, leaving him severely injured. He spent the next three months at Victoria Hospital and the day he was discharged, Jayaraj vowed to avenge the attack.

Jayaraj and his gang planned several attacks on Gopi but luck was always on the latter's side. Once they chased him down on their bikes but Gopi managed to escape. Another day, they attacked him at home but Gopi, who was trained in wrestling at the Kunjanna Garadi, managed to fight back. Jayaraj realized that he needed a better plan to launch an assault on Gopi. In desperation, he involved a policeman from the Silver Jubilee Police Station. He got the cop to summon Gopi to the police station at 2 a.m. The plan was to attack Gopi on his way back from the police station. Certain that Gopi would walk down J.C. Road, Jayaraj kept a gang of twenty-five men at hand near Kamath Hotel to attack him. However, this time too, Gopi grew suspicious and asked a relative to pick him up. The Ambassador took him to another destination instead of his home. Gopi understood that the police were acting at Jayaraj's behest and became more alert.

On the morning of 25 January 1977, Gopi was to appear in front of a magistrate for an old case. As soon as he entered the court premises, Jayaraj confronted him. He had a green shawl wrapped around him, under which he was hiding a sword. Behind Jayaraj were half a dozen men armed with sharp weapons. Before Gopi could react, Jayaraj took out his sword and slashed his chest. The drama unleashed chaos in the court, making everyone run for their lives. Gopi sought shelter in courtroom no. 2, interrupting the proceedings. Sensing danger, the advocates ran away while the judge fled into his antechamber. Another judge in the neighbouring courtroom no. 4, Chandrasekaraya, witnessed the attack.

'What a shame! What a shame!' exclaimed Judge Chandrasekaraya, who in a state of shock immediately called the police to take control over the situation.

The police had all this while looked the other way as the drama unfolded in the courthouse. Jayaraj and his gang tried to escape but the police chased them down. Patri Narayana and Venkatesha, two of Jayaraj's men, were nabbed. Judge Chandrasekaraya asked Gopi to record his statement in his presence. Gopi named Jayaraj, Samson, Kiki Raja and Vasu as the perpetrators before falling unconscious. He was rushed to Victoria Hospital. In his statement, which was recorded after he regained consciousness, Gopi alleged that his treatment at the hospital was delayed as the chief minister's son-in-law M.D. Nataraj had instructed the doctors not to treat him. However, one of the doctors did not pay heed to the order. Gopi had more than fifteen deep incised wounds that required 200 stitches in a surgery that went on for six hours. As the effect of the anaesthesia wore off, Gopi opened his eyes to find two senior police officers standing in front of him, T. Srinivasulu and P. Kodanda Ramaiah, both of whom went on to become Bengaluru police commissioners. Gopi told them that he had filed several complaints against Jayaraj and had also demanded police protection but his pleas had fallen on deaf ears. Gopi's wife, Vasantha, pleaded to the police officers with folded hands and tears in her eyes for help.

'Don't let the culprits go scot-free.'

The arrested members of Jayaraj's gang were kept at the Ulsoorgate Police Station lockup. Another gang member, Ramakrishna, was also arrested. All three of them were 'worked on' by the police. They were tortured till they broke down and revealed that Jayaraj had paid a bribe of Rs 6000 to an officer from the Silver Jubilee Police Station for information about Gopi's impending court visit.

Judge Chandrasekaraya pulled up the police for the attack in broad daylight. He became a witness in the case, making it even stronger. Till then, none of the cases against Jayaraj had stood the scrutiny of the court for lack of evidence. But the attack on Gopi changed Jayaraj's fate. The police went all out to hunt him down, But by then, he had fled from the city with Samson and Kiki Raja.

Before leaving Bengaluru, Jayaraj had a heated argument with Nataraj, where the latter reprimanded him for attacking Gopi in the courtroom. Nataraj was more upset about the damage to his reputation. Jayaraj borrowed Rs 50,000 from him and left for Vidurashwatha, a quaint village located 100 kilometres from Bengaluru. On their way out of the city, they stopped at a club in Chickpete and borrowed the owner's Fiat. At Vidurashwatha village in Gauribidanur, he took shelter at the residence of a Congress MLA.

Even in Vidurashwatha, Jayaraj could not get Gopi out of his mind. He arranged for two young women to be sent to Victoria Hospital to check on Gopi. When the women came back with news that Gopi was recuperating well, Jayaraj was filled with rage.

Back in Bengaluru, the police had launched a manhunt for Jayaraj and rounded up over eighty local goons to extract information. Ultimately, one of them caved in and told the police about his hideout. A police team reached the village and raided the MLA's house. One of the policemen recognized the two young women who had come to check on Gopi in the hospital. They turned out to be the MLA's daughters. But Jayaraj had already escaped to Tirupati with his men. He then proceeded to Mysuru where he took shelter at another Congress member's house. En route, Jayaraj consulted an astrologer who told him that he would not be able to evade arrest for long. A desperate Jayaraj sent an SOS message to Urs through the Congress worker.

'Tell the police I should not be harmed in any way.'

The police squad reached Mysuru to carry out what could have been Bengaluru's first encounter killing. Just as they were closing in on Jayaraj, a message from Urs was delivered to them. They were forced to junk the department's shoot-at-sight order and instead arrest and bring him back to Bengaluru. It was the first case against Jayaraj that led to a conviction after Judge Chandrasekaraya testified against him. He was sentenced to ten years' imprisonment, bringing the production of his newspaper *Garibi Hatavo* to an abrupt halt.

* * *

Ramchandra Rao alias Kotwal Ramchandra

Jayaraj's incarceration led to a sudden vacuum in Bengaluru's crime world. Any crafty thief or robber found

space and an opportunity to grow. Ramchandra Rao
too seized this moment and graduated from threatening
couples to extorting money from brothels, hooch dens
and several other small-time businesses.

Rao, who hailed from Shimoga (present-day
Shivamogga), lived in Malleshwaram with his family.
The Raos were Marathas but had flawlessly adopted
south Indian ways. The Marathas had found their feet
in south India way back in the 1600s when the Sultan
of Bijapur began sending expeditions to the south. The
Bijapur army, which included Shahaji Raje Bhonsle,
father of the great Maratha warrior Shivaji, managed to
capture the Bangalore Fort after a battle that went on
for three days. Since then, several Maratha families were
scattered in different parts of Karnataka.

Rao, a religious man, would regularly visit the Ishwara
temple in Malleshwaram with his mother. A school
dropout, he loved bikes since his teenage years. He even
purchased a Yamaha 350 soon after joining the Navy
as a Class-IV worker. But he found the job monotonous
and quit after a brief stint. He soon ran away, unaware
that his family would loathe such a decision. His parents
refused to take him back, which ultimately led to his
entry into the crime world.

Cut off from his family and without any financial
support, Rao started to dabble in all sorts of antisocial
activities. The six-footer, with a baritone voice, began
with petty crimes such as stealing footwear of devotees
from outside temples. Soon, he graduated to stealing
bicycles and motorcycles. Before long, Rao was involved

in several break-ins, thefts and robberies, which earned him the moniker of 'Robbery King of Bengaluru'.

There are two stories that people remember about how Rao got his alias 'Kotwal'. According to one version, after being thrown out of his house, Rao took to eating free food at *kalyan mandapas* (wedding halls) by posing as a guest. Kannadigas call such freeloaders *kottu* and soon people started calling him Kotwal. But Kotwal himself had a different story. He bragged that Urs fondly called him Kotwal and that name stayed with him.

From robberies he went on to form a small gang of thugs that would extort from illegal chit funds and brothels. But Kotwal derived a perverted pleasure in looting young couples at secluded spots. He and his men would also sexually assault the women they accosted at such spots. A senior police officer, who once raided a shanty that Kotwal had inhabited for a while, recalled finding there more than twenty brassieres. His perverted nature was ascertained years later when the police while questioning his two wives, Lilavati and Shaila, learnt that he would force them to watch porn films.

Retired policeman B.K. Shivaram, who had closely dealt with rowdies, remembered Kotwal as someone who could strike fear in the hearts of people with his muscle power. He found Kotwal cunning and intelligent.

As he gained notoriety, many people in Bengaluru hired his services to threaten or to get houses and plots vacated. A middle-aged man once approached him to evict his tenant from his bungalow in Shakarpura. The tenant was an orthodox Brahmin military colonel who lived with his family on a meagre rent and threatened the owner with his contacts every time he was asked to vacate. The hapless owner had heard about Kotwal and approached him. Kotwal's minions warned him against taking on a military man but he was fearless. He gathered every bit of information about the occupant and his family, and devised a plan that did not involve any physical harm. One day, he gave Rs 200 to a gang member and sent him to Nandi Hills, a thick patch of forested area near Bengaluru, to do a peculiar task. The man had to catch two owls. He got in touch with a member of a local tribe, known for selling fruits and medicinal herbs near the forest, to capture the birds.

Television was still a novelty in Bengaluru back then. One Saturday, when the colonel and his family were glued to their television set, Kotwal jumped over the compound wall and released the birds into the house through the kitchen window. Within a week, the tenants left the bungalow with bag and baggage, not even bothering to lock the doors.

Kotwal charged a hefty sum of Rs 20,000 for the task, which the owner readily paid.

Kotwal had thought of the plan after learning that the colonel was an orthodox Brahmin, who considered owls to be a bad omen. The colonel grew restless as the owls flew around the house. His astrologer told him it was no longer safe to stay there and that someone from his family could die. In no time, the house was vacated.

Taking advantage of Jayaraj's absence, Kotwal attempted to befriend Urs. By this time, he had started ruling Bengaluru. His coffers were flowing with mamool pouring in from numerous sources. He also changed the way criminal gangs conducted themselves. Distinct from the erstwhile gangs that moved around in autorickshaws, Kotwal's was a biker gang. The men sported yellow metal Rado watches and thick gold chains with tiger-nail pendants. Kotwal himself wore these accessories and encouraged his gang members to flaunt the same. When he was pleased with a member, he would gift him a Rado that cost over Rs 10,000.

Kotwal himself had graduated to a Royal Enfield Bullet. He also owned a Fiat in which he drove around listening to devotional songs of Sri Raghavendra Swamy. His gang had spread its tentacles across the city's length and breadth, with a robust information network to identify potential extortion targets.

During his free time, Kotwal watched kabaddi tournaments and later walked up to the players of the winning team and patted their backs. Kotwal also had a penchant for cleanliness. He would always dress immaculately in a pair of crisp trousers and shirt that he would change twice a day. He could almost pass for a sophisticated, god-fearing, well-behaved man, with a decent job. But closer interactions would expose his gruesome side. His gang members feared his wrath. There was no guarantee what would trigger him to bring out his machete. If his prized Bullet didn't come to life with one kick, he would fly into a rage and his wrath would know no bounds.

* * * *

Shiva Kumar alias Boot House Kumar alias Oil Kumar

Anyone who knew Shiva Kumar in his early days would have hardly guessed that one day he would rule Bengaluru's underworld through sheer intelligence. Born in a humble household in Akkipete, Shiva Kumar was never really interested in academics. He dropped out of school midway. His father Allappa ran a shoe shop named Lucky Boot House in Chickpete near the Raghavendra temple, which made enough money to feed a family of seven people. Shiva Kumar, who was the second of five children, spent most of his time loitering in the area with his friends. The group's favourite joint was the Govindraju Military Hotel, which was famous for its biryani. Shiva Kumar even waited tables to make some quick money.

The family's shoe shop was later run by Shiva Kumar's elder brother, Vishwanath, who was an active participant in the Kannada language movement. In 1975, Vishwanath died of a heart attack in Mysuru and the responsibility of the shop fell on Shiva Kumar's shoulders. He renamed the shop American Boot House and soon people started calling him 'Boot House Kumar'.

Shiva Kumar had a few close friends in the area, among whom was a man named Sampat. Everyone knew that Sampat dabbled in the oil dhanda but no one had a clue as to what he did exactly. But Sampat's prosperity convinced his friends, including Shiva Kumar, that it was a good business.

People hardly knew anything about oil theft back in the 1970s. Companies like Indian Oil and Burmah Oil had recently set up large-scale terminals in the city, which led to an influx of oil tankers. Small-time miscreants, drug addicts and alcoholics would steal diesel and petrol from fuel tankers coming to the city. They would stop the tankers, hold the driver at knifepoint and fill gallons of fuel to sell in the black market. A few hundred rupees were enough to buy them a week's quota of drugs, alcohol and food. Sampat, though, went a step ahead. Initially his gang of hooligans would beat up tanker drivers and steal the fuel. But soon he realized that the same could be done by simply bribing the driver. Sampat's men then progressed to taking the driver into confidence by paying him a few hundred bucks and stealing as many gallons as they wanted, without creating a scene. On the rare occasions when drivers would oppose such an arrangement, the men would resort to violence.

His weekly collection crossed Rs 2 lakh, which Sampat would distribute equally among his members while keeping the lion's share for himself. With money pouring in abundantly, Sampat planned his first international trip in the mid-1970s. He entrusted Shiva Kumar with the reins of his business, briefing him on every nitty-gritty and ways to deal with problem makers. Shiva Kumar readily agreed.

In the beginning, he followed Sampat's directions to the hilt. But the huge weekly moolah got the better of him. He caught hold of a few people and formed his own gang. He beat up Sampat's men and threatened them with dire consequences if they interfered with his business. Those from Sampat's gang who did not mind his betrayal were welcome to join his group.

The scheming Shiva Kumar had metamorphosed into 'Oil Kumar', an alias that stayed with him till his death. His business acumen probably came from his family's shoe shop. While he had learned the tricks of the trade, he expanded the business to a level that no one could imagine. He ensured that everyone related to his work was bribed and silenced. He had the entire police force under his thumb, and lawyers to bail him out of legal issues.

He then expanded the oil business by venturing into the theft of furnace oil. Furnace oil is a residue or a by-product of petroleum refineries used in distilleries, boilers, marine diesel engines and furnaces. For the factories in Bengaluru and its neighbouring areas that required furnace oil on a regular basis, the Indian Oil and Burmah Oil depots were the main suppliers. Tankers, with three compartments, would be loaded and then dispatched to various destinations. Oil Kumar worked in cahoots with the tanker drivers as well as with the oil inspectors in charge of loading and unloading of the oil. But thanks to Oil Kumar's perfectly orchestrated plans, a tanker that left with 36,000 litres of oil would reach the destination with only 24,000 litres. The missing litres were unloaded at Oil Kumar's multiple sheds that had come up at secluded areas on the outskirts of Bengaluru. He single-handedly managed to create an artificial scarcity of furnace oil, leaving factories with no choice but to buy it in black from him.

In no time, Oil Kumar became wealthy and needed physical protection of muscular men like Kotwal to manage his dealings. When Sampat returned a few months later, he was threatened and sidelined. By then, Oil Kumar had Kotwal on his pay roll and threatening people was a part of his daily routine. He had managed to expand his earnings to over Rs 5 lakh a week and all the ruffians were keen to have their share. At one point, Sampat created a ruckus over how his fortunes had turned, leading to a huge showdown between him and Oil Kumar. A compromise meeting was arranged near Lalbagh between Oil Kumar and all the rowdies who demanded a share in the oil business. Four equal shares were then charted out—Oil Kumar, a joint share for goons Market Raja and H.M.T. Prabha, Kotwal and others, including Sampat.

In spite of resenting Oil Kumar's hostile takeover of his business, Sampat partnered with him to make a foray into the film industry. Sampat knew that Oil Kumar had deep pockets.

Now a suit-wearing businessman, Oil Kumar started a film distribution firm called S.K.S. Film Distributors in 1982 with friend Shanta and business partner Sampat.

Well-known politician Jeevaraj Alva attended the launch of its office in Gandhi Nagar. Oil Kumar was passionate about cars and would get a new one every three months. From a bottle-green Premier Padmini, Oil Kumar upgraded to a Mercedes. He was the first underworld don to tour countries like Dubai and Singapore, and send his favourite punters too on foreign junkets.

While Oil Kumar was also married to a woman chosen by his family, Bengalureans only know about his second wife, Rita, whom he had met in Okalipuram. Rita was a small-time performer in low-budget movies. Once Oil Kumar purchased the negatives of an old film in which Rita had a semi-nude scene and burnt them to ashes. They got married at the picturesque hill station of Madikeri. The star-studded wedding was attended by popular film actor Ambareesh among other dignitaries. Soon he moved in with Rita to a plush house in Vijayanagar. He frequently travelled abroad with his new wife. But he never lost sight of the oil business that had grown exponentially. His sharp futuristic thinking also earned him the nickname of Chanakya.

* * *

Meanwhile, Jayaraj was restless in prison. His extortion business was slowly being taken over by Kotwal, who did not bat an eyelid before threatening people. There were very few left who cared to send Jayaraj's share to him in prison. He was completely oblivious to the sea change in Bengaluru's underworld since he had gone to jail. Jayaraj was also completely unaware of the blooming oil business that was earning huge kickbacks for Kotwal and his gang. He felt insecure. He wanted to break free.

5

Cabaret to Company Service

The high-heeled crowd of late 1970s' Bengaluru would step out at night to enjoy live dance performances in cabarets that had sprung up across the city. The patrons were elite, open-minded and westernized. Cabarets were already a rage in the West. In no time, these nightclubs became the talk of the town. The mystery of what it was like to be inside such clubs upped their popularity as well as their exclusivity. The cabarets in Bengaluru were heavily influenced by their Western counterparts. The decor would mostly comprise several round tables circling an elevated stage where women would dance sensuously to the beats of hit Bollywood numbers, classic English and a few Kannada item songs. Bollywood's cabaret queen Helen had just shot to fame and songs like 'oh haseena zulfon waali' from *Teesri Manzil*, 'piya tu ab toh aaja' from *Caravan*, 'duniya mein logon ko' from *Apna Desh* were among the most played. Songs that were picturized on item girls and wannabe starlets like Jyothi Lakshmi, her sister Jaymalini, Silk Smitha, Disco Shanti were also in demand. One of the peculiar highlights of the cabarets during this time was what the patrons called *nanga naach* or nude dancing. Though there was no nudity involved, the dancers would wear several layers of glittering brassieres during their performances, which they would then shed one after the other, flinging the discarded ones towards the patrons. This certainly aroused interest within the audience, but the women who took centre stage never stepped down from the elevated platform, maintaining a safe distance from the patrons.

Old-timers recall those days as a peculiar time. 'Cabaret dancers wanted to sway like Helen, the dining and drinking crowd wanted best-placed tables with a good view of the dancers, and the less fortunate wanted to catch a glimpse of the inside of a cabaret even if it was just for a night. Everyone in Bengaluru wanted a piece of pie.' The nightclubs visited by the who's who were Napoli, 3 Aces, Talk of the Town and Stay Longer. And then there were others like Blue Fox, Savera, Sona Greens, Bosco, Ching Lung and Charishma on Brigade Road.

Orthodox Kannadigas looked down upon cabarets, firmly believing that the evil Western culture was making youngsters fall prey to immorality. Local activists would often protest against the cabarets as many saw them as hubs of nefarious activities.

By early 1980s, the cabarets were at the peak of their popularity, and most were doing brisk business. Social leaders of the time felt threatened and feared that the cabaret culture was deviating the youth from the Kannada language movement.

There was a strong undercurrent to focus on the Kannada language in order to keep the culture alive. The language crusaders did not like the fact that Sanskrit was the dominant language in schools. The growing popularity of the English language left Kannada in a state of neglect in its home state. Soon there was a demand to demote Sanskrit as the first language in school. The Government of Karnataka constituted a committee led by V.K. Gokak, former vice-chancellor of Karnataka University, to analyse the ground reality of the language issue. In his report, Gokak recommended that Kannada be given the status of the first language. His recommendation was not just ignored by the government but also strongly opposed by non-Kannada-speaking minorities. Gokak's recommendation gave the language movement a boost. It further gained momentum when superstar Rajkumar jumped into the fray along with his colleagues, and started leading it. Rajkumar, who had earlier declined offers to enter politics, finally took the plunge, making language his first cause. His entry turned around the face of an agitation that many think would otherwise have died a slow death. Rajkumar's participation also brought along legions of his fans to the movement. Every film of his had a fan club to its name such as *Namma Samsara Abhimanala Sangha, Nanna Thamma Abhimanala Sangha, Sipayi Ramu Abhimanala Sangha, Dhruva Thare Abhimanala Sangha, Anuraga*

Aralithu Abhimanala Sangha. A single call from the actor would drive thousands of his fans out of their homes and on to the streets, giving momentum and mass support to the language movement. The agitation garnered so much prominence that the Karnataka government headed by Chief Minister R. Gundu Rao was forced to implement Gokak's recommendations.

The cabaret culture and the language movement ran almost parallel to each other. Kannadigas spent hours having heated discussions and debates in their drawing rooms on how Western culture was slowly permeating their society. Cabarets fell squarely into this space. The growing opposition from the people in the state and the rampant extortion by policemen began to hurt cabaret owners. It was not long before the rowdies turned their attention on the booming cabaret business. Then started recurrent brawls and threats of extortion. On the one hand, the rowdies would demand free liquor and entertainment, on the other, the police would ask for bribes to keep the show going. With the business bleeding, it was time to bring down the curtains on the cabarets in Bengaluru.

The void created by the closure of the cabarets was soon filled by live bands, where singers and musicians performed in front of eager audiences. The local singers, mostly women, would dress traditionally, and perform in the hope of catching the eye of a talent scout who could land them their lucky break. One of the first live bands in the city opened at the Bengaluru International Hotel on Race Course Road. As it gained popularity, the live band owners soon began to source young female performers from Kolkata and Mumbai.

What started as a purely musical endeavour soon turned into risqué showmanship. Women seductively served drinks and offered 'company service' to drunk patrons. Phone numbers scribbled on paper napkins were accompanied by a promise to meet outside the restaurant. Live band owners loved the formula as a woman's company kept the patrons at the club longer, leading to more business. Live bands were similar to the dance bars of Mumbai. In many ways, the financial capital rubbed off its nightlife culture on Bengaluru. Mumbai already had a cabaret-cum-striptease club at Churchgate called Blue Nile, the talk of not just the town but also the rest of the country. Several striptease shows were also held in other parts of Mumbai but Blue Nile was the most coveted. Travellers from other cities would never miss a visit, with one show costing up to Rs 80 at that time. Other popular cabarets were Albela at Colaba, Ritz at Churchgate, Maharaja at Chowpatty and Heritage at Byculla. Legend has it that Mumbai's cabaret owners feared no one. Even as the dancers stripped almost completely under focused stage lights, barring a few brawls here and there when a patron had a peg or two too many, most cabarets ran peacefully.

In 1972, Mumbai got its first dance bar, Sonia Mahal, at Nariman Point. It was a new concept where skimpily clad women would dance and serve alcohol. The owner of Sonia Mahal, a Sindhi, believed that not everyone liked to visit the red-light areas and *mujra* (courtesan) houses;

sophistication was an imperative for discerning clients. In an advertisement in an eveninger, Sonia Mahal was touted as 'heaven on earth'. Within months, it became the hang-out of Mumbai's underworld, who also made a beeline to demand protection money or *hafta* in Mumbai underworld parlance. Soon many other dance bars came up, the famous ones being Caesar's Palace on Linking Road, Pingara at Byculla and Topaz at Grant Road. They became dens of antisocial elements, which put immense pressure on the police. They had to deal with late night fights, shootouts and attacks. But the Mumbai Police too used the dance bars for making extra money. Former IPS officer-turned-lawyer Y.P. Singh had once described in an interview that the dance bars were 'breeding grounds for underworld, prostitution and drugs rackets'. 'Due to rampant corruption in the police department, it is very difficult to ensure proper operations of the dance bars and this will result in increase in crime.'

In Mumbai, the dance bars' first brush with notoriety came when a bar girl from Sonia Mahal was kidnapped and raped by Samad Khan, the notorious nephew of don Karim Lala. Around the same time, hotel owners in Bengaluru started noticing the profitability of dance bars in Mumbai. Many of them travelled to Mumbai to understand how the dance bars functioned. Gradually, many stewards and captains from Mumbai's dance bars were poached by Bengaluru businessmen who started live bands fashioned on the same lines. The Shettys from Mangaluru also spread their wings in Mumbai, eventually owning majority of the dance bars. It is estimated that of the 450-odd dance bars that thrived in Mumbai, 99 per cent were owned by the Shetty clan.

While live bands in Bengaluru provided livelihood to hundreds of women, they were also hubs of criminal activities with crooks closing deals in such places, passing on tipoffs, accepting suparis (Mumbai mobster slang for money paid to a hitman) and demanding mamool. But criminals weren't the only ones who reaped the dividends of the live bands. Cops too used them as a great source of 'under the table' income. The deadline for live bands was 11.30 p.m., but they remained open until the wee hours of the morning by bribing the cops. The women would be accommodated in tiny guest houses rented by the owners, who also took care of their safety and security. But the bad boys of Bengaluru lusted after them, which led to rampant quarrels, sexual assaults and kidnappings.

While the live bands went through various phases of moral illegitimacy, it was in the 1990s that the Bengaluru Police joined the faction of people demanding a ban on them. Sayed Nasru and his brothers, Zafru, Wasim and Zabi, along with their accomplices had created unmatched havoc in the city by kidnapping women working in live bands, raping them and robbing motorists on highways. Live band girls dreaded the gang so much that many refused to travel in the pick-up-and-drop facility offered by their employers. On the other hand, live band owners made frantic calls to the police requesting that they nab the culprits as it affected their business. The Nasru gang was named in seventy-seven cases of robbery, dacoity, murder, kidnappings and in over twenty cases of rape.

As an anti-rowdy squad was formed to track down Nasru and his gang, the police too turned critical of the live bands.

It turned out that the gang members would blindfold the victims and drive them to a secluded spot where they would rape them several times before throwing them on the roadside. The drive to these spots, it was learnt during the probe, took forty-five minutes. The squad then began tracing all secluded spots forty-five minutes from Bengaluru till they finally zeroed in on the location—a road to Tirupati (quite ironically a pilgrimage site). They traced a small house where the gang would take the girls and rape them. During a raid on the house, Nasru along with half a dozen men, including his brothers, were arrested. One would think incarceration would have taught him a lesson but years later, after he was released, Nasru started creating the same havoc till he was gunned down by a team led by Inspector B.K. Shivaram near Anekal in May 2005.

* * *

Back in the day when live bands were thriving centres of illegal activities, the increasing number of nightclubs meant good business. In jail, Jayaraj ensured that his share of mamool reached him regularly. Outside, Kotwal had spread his wings like a vulture. And then there were other smaller goons who struggled to hang around without any allegiance to the city's two big dons, but from time to time went on to extort from nightclub owners. Since Jayaraj was incarcerated, he would send his men to keep an eye on the city and ensure that his presence was felt through his unruly gang members. Kotwal, on the other hand, was a fan of nightclubs himself. He would hop from one club to another before retiring in a heavily inebriated state. The club owners did not risk refusing mamool ever. The damage to furniture, had they refused, would cost them much more. Not to mention their lives too were at stake. Altogether, Bengaluru's clubs would shell out more than Rs 50,000 daily as mamool to various gangs and corrupt police officials.

Not much later, the nightclubs of Bengaluru would give birth to a don who would go on to become one of India's most wanted men.

6

Operation Tiger

Sitting behind bars, Jayaraj persistently held on to Bengaluru, while Kotwal did his bit to tighten his grip. Caught between the two dons were Bengaluru's cops. There was an unmentioned, secret divide between them. Some owed allegiance to Jayaraj, some backed Kotwal. And then there was also a large section in the police force that was close to Oil Kumar, to ensure his name never got into the police records.

At times, heated discussions among the policemen would revolve around how they were losing control over the city. With the politicians and the dons almost always working hand in glove, the law enforcers were left with little or no choice but to take sides. A break from the criminal syndicates came in the form of chain snatchers on motorbikes. Back then, it was a novel idea, and some of the mob-weary cops turned to solving these new crimes.

Women had become wary of walking on the roads with chain snatchers not even sparing their *mangalsutras* (a necklace worn by married women). Apart from the monetary setback, the loss of a mangalsutra was also considered to be a bad omen. Many women stopped wearing jewellery altogether.

During one such snatching attempt, a woman who was riding pillion on a scooter on CMH Road in Indiranagar fell off as the thief attempted to snatch her chain. The chain snatcher too was riding pillion on a motorcycle. The woman suffered a serious head injury and remained in coma for six months at the National Institute of Mental Health and Neurosciences (NIMHANS). This incident led to an uproar among Bengalureans. The police were labelled as inefficient. Women's rights groups took to the streets shouting slogans against the police and challenging the commissioner to nab the culprits. The press wrote scathing articles about the lack of preparedness within the police department, no vigilance on roads and a near absence of an intelligence network. Worried about the public outrage against his men, Chief Minister Ramakrishna Hegde summoned police commissioner P.G. Halarnkar demanding a detailed plan to nab the criminals.

By this time, Bengaluru Police had registered fifty-two cases of chain snatching, of which forty-nine involved the theft of mangalsutras, and they were all committed by bikers. In a day, the criminals would snatch around five to six chains and then there would be a lull for about forty to fifty days. Soon they would strike again. The

FIRs from different police stations described the men as wearing different-coloured outfits every time they struck. This forced the police to suspect that it was the handiwork of a large gang.

Soon after meeting with the chief minister, Halarnkar was summoned by Governor A.N. Banerjee. Upset over the city's law and order situation, both of them came down heavily on the police chief.

Halarnkar called for an urgent meeting with the entire police force, including the traffic police.

'What is happening in the city? Women are being attacked. They don't feel safe any more. Is there no policeman in Bengaluru who has the guts to catch them?' Halarnkar thundered.

The police chief challenged the entire force. 'Wake up from your slumber. Do whatever it takes to nab the chain snatchers. As soon as they strike in a particular area, a wireless message has to be sent to everyone before registering an FIR. I want every single policeman on the streets manning important junctions when they strike.' Halarnkar called it Operation Tiger and announced a presidential medal for the policeman who nabbed the culprits. From the vagaries of Jayaraj, Kotwal and Oil Kumar, Operation Tiger was a welcome breather.

Sitting in the last row, traffic police sub-inspector B.B. Ashok Kumar of Ulsoorgate Police Station couldn't get the top cop's words out of his head.

Ashok Kumar had already made a name for himself by chasing down speeding cars and traffic signal violators. One popular tale involved him chasing down the son of an IAS officer, who was speeding around the city without wearing a helmet. His bike had a modified engine that produced an ear-splitting sound. The youngster knew that Ashok Kumar had been at his tail for a long time. Once, he called Ashok Kumar at the police station and dared him for a chase. When Ashok Kumar got out of the building, the youngster was waiting on his bike, revving it in anticipation. Without giving it a second thought, the cop hopped on his bike and started chasing him. He nabbed him, dragged him back to the police station, put him in the lockup and seized his bike. Knowing well that the IAS officer would be on his way, Ashok Kumar informed his senior of the incident. But to his surprise, the IAS officer thanked him for teaching his son a lesson.

A die-hard fan of Amitabh Bachchan's character in the film *Zanjeer*, Ashok Kumar aspired to be in the crime branch. His application for a crime branch posting was still pending when he got a chance to prove his mettle.

Halarnkar's words inspired Ashok Kumar to begin his own secret investigation. He wrote down all the details pertaining to the crime: the day, time, place, brand of motorcycle, registration numbers, in case there was an eyewitness, and descriptions of the accused. For the next few weeks, Ashok Kumar tried to distinguish a pattern in the snatching incidents till something finally struck him.

'New-moon day. The culprits always strike on or around the new-moon day,' he noted.

When they would strike, the first case would be reported from the eastern part of the city, progressing in a clockwise manner across Bengaluru to end again at the same area from where it was first reported. This suggested that the accused were entering and exiting Bengaluru from the east.

Another peculiar thing that Ashok Kumar noticed was that in each case, two of the four digits on the registration plate would be hidden. In one FIR, the vehicle number was noted as CNT 8XX2, while in another, it was CNT 84XX, and CNT XX32 in yet another one. Each FIR had a number with a different combination. Ashok Kumar concluded that the registration number was CNT 8432. This crucial lead gave him the required boost to pursue the case further but one thing still remained a mystery. The culprits were spotted in different clothes every time.

Ashok Kumar knew that the culprits—be it two men or a bigger gang—would not be striking without a weapon. He applied for special permission to get a revolver and thirty rounds, which was approved. He became the first revolver-bearing traffic policeman in Bengaluru, a rarity even today. His counterparts looked at him with envy; some made him a butt of their jokes.

Four months had passed since Operation Tiger was announced and so far there had been no success. On the cold, breezy morning of 23 October 1984, Ashok Kumar reported early on duty to make traffic arrangements near Trinity Circle on MG Road. The governor was paying a visit to the Trinity Church. It was the day of Naraka Chaturdashi, the second day of Diwali (the Hindu festival of lights). Hindu mythology has it that a demon called Narakasura was killed by the gods in a symbolic gesture of good winning over evil.

In the spirit of the season and for the festivities, most women had worn their best attires and gold jewellery. Ashok Kumar had an inkling that the snatchers could strike that day. There hadn't been a squeak from them in the past forty days, and it seemed like the perfect day to target women. After the governor entered the church for the programme at 9 a.m., Ashok Kumar started monitoring the wireless carefully. Exactly thirty minutes later, the wireless crackled into life.

'Tiger has struck! Tiger has struck! Cambridge Layout in Ulsoor.'

Ashok Kumar jumped on his Bullet and took Constable Alla Baksh with him. The wireless message had stated that the rider was wearing a blue helmet and a red T-shirt while the pillion rider was wearing a yellow T-shirt. Months of working on this case and years of chasing culprits on his bike meant that Ashok Kumar knew the city roads and bylanes like the back of his hand. For about an hour he rode around the city, eventually reaching the Kudremukh Iron Ore Corporation at Koramangala. There, he spotted a black motorcycle haphazardly speeding towards him. Looking closely, he distinguished the letters CNT on the registration plate. But the rider was wearing a black T-shirt and the one riding pillion was wearing white. Nevertheless, Ashok Kumar had a gut feeling that they were the culprits. His suspicion was confirmed when he tried to stop them but the biker veered away. Ashok Kumar promptly informed the police control room about the location and the chase began.

The biker was speeding at 80 km per hour but Ashok Kumar soon caught up with him. Riding alongside the men, he tried to grab the rider by his collar, a skill he had perfected while nabbing bikers violating traffic rules. However, the pillion rider suddenly brandished a Rambo knife, a sharp weapon with a rough edge on one side and a clean one on the other. But Ashok Kumar was quick to pull out his revolver with his left hand. He knew that using the right hand would've meant taking his hand off the accelerator. He pulled the trigger but nothing happened. Then he remembered that he had kept the first round empty, a practice he followed to ensure his children's safety in case of an accidental firing. He fired again, aiming at the wheels, but he missed. He then handed over the gun to Alla Baksh and asked him to point it at the bikers just to threaten them.

'We can't kill them. We have to catch them alive,' he screamed.

The police commissioner had reached the control room by then. He sent a message to Ashok Kumar to not let the culprits get away at any cost.

At one point, Ashok Kumar came very close to the duo. The only option now was to ram them. 'A fracture or two but they will never manage to run away,' he thought. He throttled the accelerator and rammed the snatchers' Yezdi. After the collision, while the rider's hand got stuck under the burning hot silencer of Ashok Kumar's bike, the pillion rider managed to pull himself up and began running. Ashok Kumar chased him down and during a fist fight, the man slashed Ashok Kumar's palm with the knife. A huge crowd had gathered at the scene. The police commissioner soon reached the spot. Angered by the mute crowd of spectators, the commissioner asked why they didn't help the policemen. To this, one of them replied, 'We thought it was a film shooting.'

Investigations revealed that the accused were brothers Narayana and Narendra, who hailed from Andhra Pradesh. Back home, they invested the money from the stolen gold in buying autorickshaws. They owned eleven of them. To hoodwink the police, the duo would come wearing several layers of clothing and change their T-shirts after each snatching incident.

For today's Bengaluru, policemen nabbing chain snatchers is no big deal. But back then, Ashok Kumar's daredevilry lifted Bengaluru's morale and made him an instant hero. It earned him his nickname: Tiger. And Tiger was soon going to be on the trail of Bengaluru's most notorious rowdies.

7

Garibi Hatavo Redux

Jayaraj stepped out of the District Prison of Mysore, his receding hairline now more prominent. It was 1984. His ten-year-long sentence had been reduced by a few years after pulling several strings. Prison often breaks down people but Jayaraj walked out stronger than ever. He waved at the group of one hundred men who had gathered outside the gate to greet him with cheers of 'Anna, welcome! Welcome, Anna!' The don warmly put his arm around each one of them and then sat in his white Ambassador, a sign of luxury in those days, and drove away.

Once at his Wilson Garden residence, he began to take stock of his business. His biggest strength, Devaraj Urs, was no more; his mouthpiece *Garibi Hatavo* had not seen a single print while he was in jail and Kotwal had taken over his share of the business. The last update angered Jayaraj the most. He asked one of his lawyers to pass on a very specific message to Kotwal.

'Go back to your Shimoga. Don't you dare meddle in my business.'

Kotwal was not one to budge; Jayaraj too was not known to accept defeat.

Besides regaining control of his black businesses, Jayaraj revived his ambition of becoming a messiah. He also wanted to join politics but knew that he had to first deal with the current situation. His gang members were quick to inform him about Kotwal's allegiance to Oil Kumar, who was making huge profits in the illicit oil business. The oil business was fairly new for Jayaraj, who had only extorted from nightclubs and brothels. But his gang members, Jederahalli Krishnappa, Gedda Naga, Killi Rama Krishna and others, filled him in on the booming business.

'Anna, Oil Kumar earns lakhs every week. Kotwal's share is also very high,' said one of Jayaraj's men.

Within weeks, Jayaraj's men started attacking Kotwal's gang members in order to send a clear message to Oil Kumar: his business would not be able to move forward until he paid his respects to Jayaraj. The suited oil boss soon sought a meeting with Jayaraj for a settlement, and the latter demanded a lion's share from Oil Kumar.

'Who is Kotwal? He is just a bloody roadside rowdy.'

Caught in the crossfire between Jayaraj and Kotwal, Oil Kumar hated his helplessness. But he also knew that he could not function without muscle power, something that could only come from Kotwal or Jayaraj. Oil Kumar agreed to give a huge share to Jayaraj but thoughts of killing one of the power centres never left his mind.

With his grip back on Bengaluru, Jayaraj revived the defunct All India Small and Medium Newspapers Federation and became its self-appointed president. All small-time newspaper publishers and editors would approach Jayaraj for funding and he would happily oblige. These so-called scribes would then take turns to fill Jayaraj's *Garibi Hatavo* and also ghostwrite his columns that appeared on the second page. On other days, they would publish bulletins of their own if they had money to print and anything newsworthy to report. Soon it became a regular Sunday affair for Jayaraj to call a grand meeting of the federation members at his *Garibi Hatavo* office in Gandhi Nagar and dole out cash. But journalists and editors were not the only ones who looked forward to his Sunday gaiety. Even policemen lower in the hierarchy and locals would seek his generosity. From births, weddings, naming ceremonies to last rites, Jayaraj would contribute for all such occasions without any hesitation.

During one such meeting, a journalist mentioned to Jayaraj about the World Kannada Conference, an upcoming gathering of well-known writers, poets and top government authorities, in Mysuru. The conference, first of its kind in Karnataka's history, was the brainchild of former chief minister R. Gundu Rao, but was ultimately organized when the first non-Congress chief minister Ramakrishna Hegde took over. P.S. Ramanujam, deputy inspector general of police (DIG), was himself overseeing the security arrangements of this high-profile event. Along with Hegde, other chief guests for the three-day event included renowned litterateurs K. Shivarama Karanth, Kuvempu and V.K. Gokak, the man who had spearheaded the Kannada language movement. Jayaraj learnt that the most influential people in Karnataka were on the list of attendees. So, in the winter of 1985, Jayaraj decided to crash the conference. While it seemed as if he wanted to protest against the government's neglect of small and medium newspapers, he was actually keener on getting his pictures published in the newspapers the following day. He believed that it would lend him credibility as a social activist.

However, Jayaraj's All India Small and Medium Newspapers Federation was not the only one with an agenda. There were several others who had come to vent their anger against the government. One such group of protesters was that of small-time journalist Sachiva Shridhar. Other protesters comprised groups of Dalit poets and revolutionary writers who had similar qualms. But DIG Ramanujam's stringent security arrangements ensured that the protesters were surrounded and shoved into police vehicles within fifteen minutes of their arrival at the venue. They were directly taken to an open-air jail in Mysuru. The detainees were divided into two groups: one consisting of people from the cultural world and the other comprising antisocial elements. Jayaraj's group was obviously part of the latter.

Soon the literary group began their theatrical protest in the jail reciting poems, singing songs and shouting anti-government slogans.

What kind of government is this?
This is motherless government
This is fatherless government
This is an orphaned government
Don't expect anything from this government . . .

They banged the walls, clapped and sang in high-pitched voices. Shridhar had taken the lead in sloganeering, encouraging others to join him. Jayaraj and his group sat quietly watching the drama unfold. At night, the sudden screech of a cargo tempo halted their performance. Two men swiftly began unloading boxes on the jail premises and Jayaraj's aides quickly reached out for the goodies. Such was his clout that he had arranged for several cartons of McDowell's whisky and boxes of biryani inside the jail. The treat was open to all; even the policemen participated in the feast. Jayaraj invited Shridhar to join in as well.

'Why are you sitting on the other side? Come here, join us,' Jayaraj told Shridhar, offering him a drink.

In a drunken state, the cops laid out two mats: one for the cultural group and the other for the antisocials; no pillows, no blankets, just mats. Angered by the treatment meted out to them, Shridhar yelled at one of the cops, demanding that he be allowed to speak to the DIG. The cop was probably so sloshed that he gave in to the demand and rung up Ramanujam.

'Why are we being treated like criminals? We are writers, journalists. We cannot be treated like some pickpockets,' Shridhar told Ramanujam. He demanded that beds, pillows and blankets be arranged for each one of them, including Jayaraj's men. Thoroughly impressed by Shridhar's attitude, Jayaraj sent for him soon after he returned to Bengaluru. He offered him the position of the associate editor at *Garibi Hatavo*. At that time, Shridhar ran an eponymous newspaper that was published as and when he had money. So he happily accepted Jayaraj's offer at a hefty weekly salary of Rs 2500.

Shridhar thought *Garibi Hatavo* resembled a pamphlet more than a newspaper. Jumbo-sized headlines and straplines left little space for content on the poorly designed pages. Shridhar changed the format drastically and made the 'pamphlet resemble a newspaper'. Jayaraj's name appeared as the printer, publisher and editor. The paper continued to attract readers with its sensational news and headlines. No one dared to question or protest against what appeared in the paper. Who would want to incur Jayaraj's wrath? The policemen were harrowed for being targeted constantly. Their pictures of accepting bribes, beating up people and entering brothels for extortion and self-entertainment were flashed on the front page regularly. It was as if Jayaraj avenged his hatred for the police through his newspaper.

One of the most sensational exposés of *Garibi Hatavo* was the brutal thrashing of V. Sashidhar, the president of the All Karnataka Police Mahasangha. The newspaper published pictures of a wounded Sashidhar admitted at Victoria Hospital. Sashidhar was spearheading a movement against the ill-treatment of lower-rung policemen by their seniors. The orderlies were routinely exploited and made to buy home supplies for their seniors, escort their children to school and back, and drive their families around. Sashidhar, who was being constantly pressurized to shut down the union, was attacked by unknown men at allegedly the behest of senior police officers. Shridhar was the first one to visit the hospital, interview him and take his pictures. The brain behind the story was, of course, that of Jayaraj.

With his newspaper in able hands, Jayaraj now had bigger things to worry about. His share of money coming from Oil Kumar had reduced drastically over the past few months. Kotwal had not budged despite the warnings and continued to meddle in all his businesses. He summoned Oil Kumar and demanded that the protection money be given to him entirely. Oil Kumar sounded apologetic and said he was helpless.

'Anna, what do I do? I just want to run my business peacefully. I cannot afford to cut off Kotwal completely as that would make him very angry,' he told Jayaraj. On the other hand, he convinced Kotwal that Jayaraj was a nagging cause of worry.

Kotwal continued to enjoy the stardom that he had discovered when Jayaraj was away. Using the clout of a politician, he made the General MLA Hostel his permanent residence. He moved around the city with a motorcade. He also chose his men carefully after assessing their height and physique; a broad-chested, six-footer stood more chances of being a part of his gang.

The enmity between Jayaraj and Kotwal was so intense that the gang members' drunken banter would only revolve around one topic: who would get killed first? Bets were laid secretly on Kotwal and Jayaraj, even as the dons themselves plotted to eliminate each other. The smaller gangs would often get together to discuss on whose side they would be if things got hotter between the dons and the fight spilled on to the streets. But amid these hush-hush discussions and the anticipation of a full-fledged bloodbath, something very unusual happened. Kotwal sent his men to Jayaraj with an offer of a 'compromise meeting' and to everyone's surprise, Jayaraj agreed. The agenda was clear: to settle the share of all businesses, mainly that of the multi-crore oil business.

Jayaraj had an inkling that something was not quite right. But he agreed for one reason: he wanted to concentrate on the makeover of his public image; he didn't want to be known as a goon. If an agreement could be worked out, Kotwal and he would probably function in peace, he thought. After much deliberation, a meeting was fixed at Hotel Kanishka in Gandhi Nagar on 3 January 1986. The small restaurant-cum-lodge was a neutral choice. It was neither Jayaraj's hang-out nor Kotwal's. The hotel, close to the city's railway station, was popular among travellers who spent a night or two there before embarking on their journey ahead.

A fortnight before the meeting, Kotwal summoned all the rowdies on his pay roll. His gang of fifty seasoned criminals included Amanulla alias Bachchan, Bomb Krishnamurthy and his man Friday Seetharam Shetty. He announced that they had a 'big assignment' coming up and he wanted all of them to be prepared.

'We have to kill one *gandu*. He has become a pest,' Kotwal announced.

No one dared to ask who the target was, or how he looked or even why he had become a pest. As the D-Day came closer, the gang began collecting machetes, knives and swords that were called *longs*. Shawls too were bought in bulk to hide the weapons. On the day of the attack, the gang spread out, hiding behind bushes and parked cars in the compound of the hotel. Faces covered by monkey caps and shawls hiding weapons underneath, the rowdies waited patiently for the clock to strike eight. But as the cold wind blew, Kotwal became impatient and ordered one of his minions to get everyone some booze. By the time the sun set, the gang was already in high spirits.

Sharp at 8 p.m., Jayaraj walked into the gated compound, unaware of what was awaiting him. Jayaraj's office was a few blocks away and he had unsuspectingly come on foot, only with his close aide Samson in tow. As soon as Jayaraj entered, Kotwal signalled his gang.

'Attack this gandu!' he screamed, closing in on Jayaraj with his machete. His gang members followed him but as soon as they saw Jayaraj, they froze. Some of the men could only make feeble attacks on Samson. Jayaraj gathered himself and kicked Kotwal hard before running for his life inside the hotel. Through the kitchen, a tiny staircase led to the lodge above. Jayaraj escaped to the lodge and locked himself inside a room. Through the window, he watched the entire drama unfold in the compound. With his gang members giving up one after the other, Kotwal had no courage left to confront Jayaraj, let alone attack him. He and the remaining gang members fled on their motorcycles. A standby car, which Kotwal was supposed to jump into post the attack, also left the compound. Alerted by Samson, Jayaraj's gang members had by then arrived in large numbers to save their boss.

Maddened after the failed attack, Kotwal and his gang went on a rampage on their motorcycles in Gandhi Nagar, smashing cars, vandalizing shops and even attacking two innocent passers-by.

Meanwhile, Jayaraj was seething with anger. He could not come to terms with the fact that he had walked into such an obvious trap. As soon as Kotwal and his men left, Jayaraj stepped out and headed straight to the police station to file a complaint. The Kanishka attack was registered with the police. In the crime world, those who participated in the attack with Kotwal were labelled as daring rowdies. After all, who else would agree to fatally attack Jayaraj?

With Jayaraj's clout, a special anti-rowdy squad was formed to nab Kotwal. The squad consisted of six policemen with large informer networks, sharp knowledge of the functioning of the rowdies and expertise in 'breaking' or 'working' on the culprits. 'Breaking' or 'working' in police jargon meant the worst kind of torture that made the accused eventually sing.

But the investigators hit a dead end when they learnt that Kotwal had been lodged in Madanapalle jail in Andhra Pradesh at the time of the attack. How was that even possible? Only Kotwal's closest aides knew the full story.

Fearing murder charges, Kotwal had paid his sources and got himself arrested by the local police in Madanapalle well before the attack. The charges were that he was moving suspiciously in the area. The Madanapalle police promptly registered a complaint and took his hand- and foot-prints, photographs, made a MOB card and presented him before a magistrate. Kotwal was then remanded to judicial custody. But here's where he tricked everyone. He managed to find an impersonator of similar height and build and sent him to jail instead. One of his advocates, who had planned the jail stunt, asked Kotwal why his presence was so crucial at the time of the attack. He would anyway be a prime suspect and his presence would only make the case stronger.

'My boys will not have the guts to kill the Maharaja without me,' Kotwal reasoned.

In a strange sense of acceptance, Kotwal like many others addressed Jayaraj as Maharaja or 'great king'. A few days after the failed attack, Kotwal returned to his room at the General Hostel, restless. He knew that Jayaraj would not spare his life. The failed attempt had also dealt a blow to his stature. But what bothered him the most was being ridiculed and mistrusted in the crime world for attempting to turn a compromise meeting into a massacre. The crime world too was governed by a set of rules and ethics. Rowdies may be involved in the most heinous crimes but trust was a non-negotiable rule that had to be honoured at any cost. With the Kanishka incident, the gangs of Bengaluru labelled Kotwal as the most deceitful don.

All major incidents of crime in Bengaluru were recorded in a report that every police station sent to senior officers, including the deputy commissioners of police and the police commissioner. The police express reports first landed on the desk of the police clerk before being handed over to the deputy commissioners and finally to the commissioner. On the day of the Kanishka attack, a detailed report reached the commissioner. It talked about the failed attempt on Jayaraj's life as well as the official complaint registered against Kotwal. The report mentioned that Jayaraj had escaped the attack unhurt while one of his gang members had suffered injuries.

Back home in Vijayanagar, Oil Kumar was fuming as he held a copy of the express report. He paced angrily from one end of the house to the other. Much before the express reports reached the commissioner, they reached Oil Kumar, the man whose tentacles had the entire city in a vice-like grip. Kotwal was simply the executor; the brain behind the Kanishka attack was that of Oil Kumar's.

8

Rebel Rowdies: Rise of the New Breed

In the year 1974, Sreedhar Murthy, a thin, frail young man aspiring to study law, arrived in Bengaluru. In a sudden twist of fate, he turned into a notorious law-breaker.

Born on 20 March 1955 in a town called Madanayakanahalli, about fifty miles from Bengaluru, Sreedhar was an avid reader since childhood. Some said he would devour storybooks even before he turned seven. But his schoolmates had little regard for his knowledge on all things under the sun. They ribbed him for being frail and called him 'Kaddi Pehelwan'. Sreedhar ignored the jibes throughout his teen life but secretly vowed to work on his frame. At eighteen, he began exercising to build a stronger physique and silence those who had ridiculed him.

After finishing college in Kanakpura, Sreedhar came to Bengaluru to study law before preparing for the civil service examinations. He enrolled at the Vokkaligara Sangha Law College and secured accommodation at the institution's hostel. The college was run by the Vokkaliga community. Sreedhar's literary spark and a bulky stack of books in his hostel room created an erudite aura around him. Fellow students looked up to him and were in awe of his command over English language. Sreedhar himself took great pride in it. He flaunted his personal library in the hostel room, where works of French philosophers Albert Camus and Jean-Paul Sartre, books by Franz Kafka and several others adorned the shelves.

After attending lectures in the morning, Sreedhar would hang out with a select few friends in the hostel. He would spend a few hours in the gymnasium every day and on some days, he would visit a relative in Jnana Bharathi at Bengaluru University to discuss and debate on topics related to literature. The university was frequented by several poets and writers and Sreedhar had befriended most of them.

At that time, Jayaraj's punters were spread all over. The students would often discuss two men who were on Jayaraj's pay roll and active in the area, Mohammaden Block Ali and Razor Vasu. Through an acquaintance, Sreedhar befriended Vasu, who went on to become his first friend in the crime world. Sreedhar would often tag along with Vasu in an autorickshaw as the latter set out to extort money, armed with a sharp razor to threaten his targets. Through Vasu, Sreedhar befriended Ali.

The Emergency was at its peak when Sreedhar met noted Kannada journalist P. Lankesh, a man of many

talents. He dabbled in poetry, fiction writing, playwriting
and film-making. Lankesh was working on a film called
Anurupa and was in the process of finalizing the cast.
He offered a small role to Sreedhar, who readily agreed.
Lankesh also asked Sreedhar to look for another man
who could play the part of a thug. The next day, Sreedhar
introduced Lankesh to Ali, who too was promptly signed
for the role. Sreedhar enjoyed his proximity to antisocials
like Vasu and Ali as much as he liked to hobnob with
intellectuals.

After completing his acting assignment, Sreedhar left
for New Delhi in 1977 to appear for the civil services
examination. Failing to clear it, he returned six months
later and re-established contact with Lankesh.

Sreedhar's entry into the crime world was precipitated
after he beat up a young boy accused of stalking Lankesh's
daughter. In another incident that took place a little later,
a man named Bhasker was found dead in Basavanagudi.
The previous day, Bhasker had had an altercation with
Sreedhar, which led the police to suspect him. Though
he came out clean, these two incidents drove a wedge
between him and Lankesh and Sreedhar's visits to the
renowned writer reduced gradually.

By this time, Sreedhar had acted in six movies. The
brush with the silver screen inspired him to become
a film-maker but money was a problem. He sought
a loan from a bank in Mangaluru. It was 1979 and
India was playing against Pakistan in a test match at
the M. Chinnaswamy Stadium in Bengaluru. Sreedhar's
brother, Basanth, a huge cricket fan, had managed to

get tickets for the game and had come down to the city from Kanakpura. When Basanth was on his way home from the stadium at night, five men attacked him with swords and machetes. Basanth collapsed in a pool of blood. He was admitted to Victoria Hospital with grave injuries. Sreedhar, who was in Mangaluru for bank work, rushed back.

'Who was it, Basanth?' Sreedhar asked, his tone laced with anger. Basanth had no clue except that the attackers had repeatedly asked him if he was Hariprasad's man.

'Annaiah, I don't know any Hariprasad,' Basanth told Sreedhar.

The next morning Sreedhar went to the Basavanagudi Police Station to lodge a complaint. But instead, the sub-inspector instigated Sreedhar to hunt down the attackers and chop them into pieces. Sreedhar was taken aback by the cop's response. He returned to the hospital and stared at his injured brother without uttering a word.

Later that day, Sreedhar activated his contacts to find out who was behind the attack. Finally, one name reached him. The men were from Robbery King Kotwal's gang. Sreedhar had never heard of Kotwal before. Most of his small-time rowdy friends were unaware of Kotwal's existence. But a few of them who had heard stories about his notoriety knew that Kotwal was danger personified. It turned out that Kotwal's men were on a crazy crime spree trying to hunt down a man named Hariprasad and his friends. Basanth was simply a case of mistaken identity. Nevertheless, Sreedhar was determined not to take the attack lying down.

'Kotwal Ramchandra will pay for what he has done to my brother. I will kill him,' twenty-four-year-old Sreedhar promised himself.

For the rest of his life, Sreedhar would blame the attack on his brother for pushing him into the underworld. But a closer look at his life's story tells otherwise. While Basanth recovered within a month and went on to become a police officer, Sreedhar sank deeper into the world of crime.

He started collecting information about Kotwal from every small crook he knew. He began befriending many of them and even started assembling his own group of loyalists, mostly rowdies who held grudges against Kotwal. All of them wanted to see him dead. But tracing the notorious don was not an easy task. Kotwal was extremely suspicious of everyone around him. He not only slept in different locations every night, but one of his trusted aides would always be on the vigil wherever he slept. Sreedhar and his gang chalked out several plans to eliminate Kotwal but they always hit a dead end because the information about Kotwal's whereabouts would invariably turn out to be false or dated.

By now, Sreedhar knew that he was drawn irresistibly to the dark alleys, an experience he had begun to enjoy. But to sustain his hunt for Kotwal, Sreedhar had to think of ways to make money. He started committing petty crimes on the streets.

From snatching wrist watches to grabbing wallets, Sreedhar had become a pro at threatening people. He slowly graduated to recovery assignments where he and his minions would beat up people to extort money. They were not big names in the underworld and therefore had to settle for small tasks to earn money.

In the 1980s, renting videocassette recorders (VCRs) and television sets to watch movies was a rage. Sreedhar and his gang would rent VCRs and sell them. If the VCR vendor ever managed to catch hold of them, they would beat him black and blue. They also made money through cheating counterfeit currency sellers. Sreedhar and his men would identify the fake note sellers in several parts of the city and catch hold of them. After a few friendly deals, Sreedhar and gang would find the location of the main den and loot all the real money from the counterfeit sellers. The gang made large amounts through the counterfeit sellers, assured of no police involvement in the matter as the 'victims' were law-breakers themselves. Gradually, Sreedhar, who had great social skills, started meddling in settlement of land disputes. But in the bargain, he lost all his old friends from college and the literary circle, who distanced themselves from him.

Around the same time, Sreedhar got an assignment from a Hindu businessman who was cheated by a Muslim to the tune of Rs 5 lakh. Sreedhar sought his friend Sardar's help to resolve the matter. But Sardar put him in touch with Sayed Aman alias Bachchan, a small-time criminal from Banashankari, as he believed that a Muslim could help out Sreedhar better. Bachchan, who was six foot two, was a daring rowdy. His striking resemblance to Bollywood superstar Amitabh Bachchan had made him immensely popular. The son of a policeman from Tumkur, Bachchan had shifted to Bengaluru with his family after his father's retirement. He bought an autorickshaw to earn a living and look after his family. But the man he purchased the vehicle from duped him of his money. This acted as a trigger, spurning Bachchan to carry out petty crimes instead of earning money through honest means. When Bachchan and Sreedhar met, they instantly struck a cord and have since then remained partners in crime. They are still known as the only Hindu–Muslim pair in the crime world, who have remained good friends.

Five years had passed since Sreedhar swore to avenge the attack on his brother. Lankesh's tabloid, *Lankesh Patrike*, had published several articles on Kotwal. Someone suggested that it would be a good idea to facilitate a meeting between Lankesh and Kotwal. Sreedhar jumped at the idea and through Sardar finally managed to meet Kotwal. The don came on his Yamaha 350cc motorcycle a few minutes after his minions recced the place and ruled out any danger. Sreedhar noticed his thick gold chain, bracelet and Rado watch. The meeting between the two was cordial. Sreedhar knew that he would have to wait for the right time to attack him.

* * *

In Puttur, Karnataka's Dakshin Kannada district, two people fought over the produce of a jackfruit tree. To settle the matter, they went to Nettala Muthappa Rai. He hacked the tree and ended the fight.

Born in 1953, Rai grew up in a house that was always teeming with people. His father, a panchayat head, would settle disputes in Puttur. On any given day, his mother would serve coffee to not less than fifty people. While growing up, Rai always wondered why so many people crowded into his house every day.

'Why can't the problems be solved quickly? Why do we have to waste so much coffee over them every single day?' he would ask his mother.

A conservative panchayat head, Rai's father would take months to settle cases. Before pronouncing his verdicts, he would patiently hear both sides and ensure there was no injustice done to either of the parties. Rai, who grew up observing his father closely, didn't quite like his sluggish ways of delivering justice. On days when his father would be away, Rai would step into his shoes and offer a quick redressal. But his father did not approve of his ways and found his decisions hasty. He got his son, an arts graduate, a clerical job at Vijaya Bank in Puttur to keep him away from home. But Rai took a liking to the sense of importance he got as a leader. At the bank, he got involved in issues outside the purview of his duty. When the bank was sparring with the employees' union, Rai offered support to the bank management and took charge of the situation. Since then, he always remained the management's go-to man. His good looks combined with an impressive personality earned him the moniker 'hero of Vijaya Bank' from some of his colleagues.

But his father began to worry as he got more and more entangled in management and union disputes. Rai was hardly doing any real bank work. His tasks were carried out by his colleagues either out of respect or due to fear. Rai took home merely Rs 500 to Rs 600 out of his monthly remuneration of Rs 2500 since most of his days were marked as 'leave without pay' as he remained busy with out-of-office affairs. Miffed, his father insisted that he seek a transfer to Bengaluru. Rai surprisingly and readily agreed to it.

In Bengaluru, Rai met and fell in love with an attractive woman named Reca. But their families did not accept the relationship as Rai belonged to the Bunt community and Reca was a Coorgi. The couple eloped and got married in a court in Mumbai, where Rai had got a transfer and worked at the bank's Gamdevi, Wadala and Fort branches. Little had changed as he continued to stay involved in management issues more than official work. During his short stint in Mumbai, Rai managed to get noticed by one of the underworld dons who even offered him a job. But Rai refused. Struggling to make ends meet in the expensive city, Rai decided to return to Puttur with his wife and their firstborn, Rocky. Rai's ageing parents forgot their anger when he walked in with their grandchild.

The Puttur Police Station was merely ten blocks from Vijaya Bank and like all small towns, everybody knew everybody. The police officers knew all the residents, their occupations, conduct and every little detail that they would otherwise struggle to find out in big cities like Bengaluru. Lava Kumar, a strict sub-inspector, was posted in the town. His regard for law-abiding citizens and harshness towards wrongdoers had made him extremely popular in a short span of time. He went from one school to another talking to children about crime and traffic rules. The children took his discussions back home and the entire town knew about him. Among the many people he chatted up with was Rai. Lava Kumar recalls that there was nothing striking about him. He was like any other ordinary office-going man. He was probably the first police officer to become friends with Rai. When an invitation was extended, Lava Kumar also attended the birthday party of Rai's son. He was transferred many times and years later he investigated a murder case implicating Rai.

Rai was a loyalist of the Bharatiya Janata Party (BJP) that had a strong hold on Puttur. But when one of his close friends was contesting elections on a Congress ticket and asked Rai for support, he chose to stand by him. Half the BJP supporters sided with Rai, which helped his friend win comfortably with 25,000 votes. The grand victory—a first for Congress in Puttur—led to several clashes between the two parties. There were seven cases registered against Rai. He had no choice but to once again relocate to Bengaluru, where his life was set to take a dramatic turn.

Once a man walked up to Rai in the bank and made him an offer to run a cabaret on Brigade Road. Rai brushed aside the deal saying he had no money. But he accepted the offer excitedly when he was explained that he wouldn't have to make any investment. His sole responsibility would be to manage the rowdies who created a nuisance by demanding mamool. The monotony of the bank job had failed to satiate his craving for an edgy life. An even bigger incentive was that of earning daily rather than depending on a fixed monthly salary.

The cabaret required some structural changes and lighting that would cost around Rs 80,000 to Rs 1 lakh. Rai convinced an old man to become his partner and invest his money for repairs. The cabaret was named Omar Khayyam in the year 1984. It was a time when Bengaluru's cabarets and live bands were at the peak of their popularity. And like most Bunts who aspired to make it big in the hotel business, Rai walked down the same path. It was here that Rai would have his first real encounter with the crime world.

The dancers who worked at Omar Khayyam stayed at the nearby Rose Guest House, which was managed by a man named Nagesha. The women were carefully picked for the job. They had to be fair-skinned with the right amount of oomph. Shy and not-so-voluptuous women were rejected outright. As the business grew, Rai also transitioned from a regular clerk who wore slippers to work to a suited-booted man with a cabin to himself inside the cabaret, where he handled all the cash. He stepped out only to intervene in big problems.

His booming business was soon noticed by some goons from the Koli Faiyaz gang of Shivajinagar. Six men accosted Rai one night and demanded mamool. Rai refused without batting an eyelid.

'There is no way I am going to pay you bastards. Go away and threaten someone else!' he yelled at them.

But the gang was persistent and threatened him with dire consequences. Rai punched one of them in the face and hurled abuses at the other. Within seconds, Rai's force of a dozen men appeared and overpowered the gang. Rai had hired several hefty men from Dakshin Kannada district. The small-time rowdies of the Koli Faiyaz gang were no match for such a burly opposition. A few punches and some more expletives later, they ran for their lives.

'We will see you later. We will not leave you. Don't assume this is over,' they threatened Rai before leaving.

Rai's daring defence had become the talk of the nightclubs. The businessmen from the Bunt community were regularly suffering losses due to demands of extortion. He became a hero overnight for them. His defiant act was the talking point among the extortionists.

The hubs of nightclubs, Brigade Road and MG Road, had become problem areas that would see violence and brawls almost every other night. Rowdies from all gangs would loiter in the area to extort money, harass the club dancers and demand free food and booze. But Rai's army changed everything. Men from Jayaraj's, Kotwal's and Koli Faiyaz's gangs would be beaten up as soon as they created any trouble. The culprits would then be handed over to the police. Rai inadvertently donned the mantle of a protector for the nightclub owners and the ruffians did not dare to venture on Brigade Road and MG Road. He did not care which gang he picked a fight with. Rai treated everyone with equal contempt.

Once a group of seven rowdies tried to enter Omar Khayyam. There was a ticketed entry of Rs 50, which the men refused to pay. When the guard stopped them, they called for the manager. Rai emerged from his tiny cabin and walked up to the gate.

'What is all this ruckus about?'

'Let us in. Do you know who we are? How dare this guard ask us for tickets?' said one of the rowdies.

'This is not a *dharamshala*. We need money to run it,' Rai replied.

To this, one of the rowdies showed off several scars on his body, saying, 'You know who I am? I am Kaala from Gandhi Nagar.'

'You low-life! I will come and hit you in Gandhi Nagar!'

Rai's audacious behaviour helped the business flourish to a great extent. Rich men, who in the past were targeted and looted after they visited a club, could now come to Omar Khayyam without fear.

Rai now had a revolver that he flashed every time things went out of control. He would justify his actions saying: 'I do it for my living.'

One day, a rowdy named Zarar created a ruckus inside Omar Khayyam. He picked up a chair to hit Rai. In a flash, Rai took out his revolver and pointed it at Zarar's forehead. Zarar, who hadn't in his wildest imagination expected to have a gun being brandished in his face, started shivering. He was mercilessly beaten up by Rai's men. With every new tale, the crime world only got more and more curious about the gutsy owner of Omar Khayyam.

* * *

Sreedhar and Rai were contemporaries in the crime world though their paths did not cross for a very long time. They were pursuing their respective enemies till circumstances brought them together.

9

Bengaluru's Dongri: Genesis of the Muslim Mafia

India's most wanted gangster Dawood Ibrahim started out as a petty thief and bootlegger in the bylanes of Dongri, a congested Muslim-dominated area in South Mumbai. His ascent to the world of crime added to the notoriety of 'Mumbai–400009', a pin code synonymous with the neighbourhood, infamous for gangsters Karim Lala and Yusuf Batla, who once frequented its streets.

The choked gullies and gridlocked streets of Dongri continue to be a haven for pickpockets, drug peddlers and a nightmare for the Mumbai Police. Like Mumbai's Dongri, Bengaluru had Shivajinagar, the birthplace of the Muslim mafia. There were many thugs in the area but the one who was shaping up to be the most notorious was Faiyaz Ahmed.

Faiyaz, the third of seven siblings, was born into a poor family of poultry workers. His father Amirjaan, who worked in a chicken shop in Shivajinagar, could barely make ends meet. With his meagre earnings, he could only provide his children with food and shelter but no education. Amirjaan's only dream was to see his five sons grow up and start working so that they could add to the family's income and marry off their two younger sisters. But Amirjaan always knew that Faiyaz was the strongest of the lot. At the age of fifteen, when Faiyaz would join his father at work, he would single-handedly pick up a cage full of fifty hens. This motivated Amirjaan to send Faiyaz to a garadi mane to train in traditional wrestling. While the entire family survived on basic food, Amirjaan ensured that Faiyaz got his quota of nutrition, which included two litres of milk every day. He also kept a supply of eggs handy from his poultry shop to satiate Faiyaz's hunger pangs. Much to his father's delight, Faiyaz was passionate about his daily *kasrat* and went on to build a solid body. With his muscle power, his brashness too escalated with each passing day.

Faiyaz, sixteen then, had badly beaten up a local ruffian named Chulku Munna near Sangeet Theatre in Shivajinagar. The news spread like wildfire. Amirjaan, however, did not want his son's image to get tainted. He had big dreams for him. He wanted Faiyaz to participate in wrestling competitions and win prizes. He thought Faiyaz was the best bet for the family to resolve their financial troubles. He pushed Faiyaz into a serious bodybuilding regime. The teenager would exercise from 4 a.m. to 7 a.m. and then practise wrestling from 4 p.m. to 7 p.m., a routine that he never broke. By the time he turned twenty-five, Faiyaz had already won ten kushti competitions in Mysuru. But his calling lay elsewhere.

The *pehelwani* competitions hardly brought home any money for the family. Unlike what Amirjaan had imagined, the fame of his son's sport was limited to the day of the bout. Their lives remained the same and so did their financial status. Restless to make it big, Faiyaz started running the poultry shop in Russell Market and learnt the tricks of the trade. But the petty earnings from the shop left him dissatisfied. At that time Chudi Pehelwan and his aide Sarkar Pehelwan reigned over half a dozen garadis in Shivajinagar. They wielded muscle power to collect mamool from shopkeepers. Faiyaz, who was a regular at the garadi, looked up to Chudi Pehelwan and considered him a mentor. Taking a cue from his guru's business model, Faiyaz too started extorting money by flexing his muscles. In no time, money began pouring in.

Faiyaz started to command the kind of power notorious smuggler Ahmed Khan alias Baashu Dada did in Mumbai. The don from Mumbai's Teli Mohalla was known for his love for bodybuilding. Baashu Dada's bulging biceps were enough to intimidate anyone, a trait that Faiyaz was trying to use as well. While Baashu Dada progressed to dealing in gold and silver, his match in Bengaluru had found a unique way to make big money.

In the late 1970s, Bengaluru witnessed a boom of non-vegetarian eateries run by Muslim migrants from Kerala. These hotels were colloquially known as 'Kakka hotels'—Kakka being a slang term to address people from Kerala. Among the most popular Kakka hotels were Empire and Imperial. Around the same time, luxury hotels such as Ashoka, Windsor Manor and Stay Longer also came up in the city, serving a wide range of non-vegetarian dishes. The meat served in all these hotels came from Russell Market in Shivajinagar.

Faiyaz chalked out a plan. He closely studied the business models of the other shops and the prices they offered and came up with his own strategy to rule the market. He demanded that all poultry dealers supply only to him and to no one else.

'No one will directly deal with any hotels,' he announced. 'If you do, be ready to face the consequences.'

He had formed a small gang of hooligans to threaten and beat up any shop owner who did not abide by his diktat. The hotel owners felt helpless as every day the gang members would disperse in the area and keep an eye on the shopkeepers. The hotel owners had no choice but to purchase their stock from Faiyaz exclusively. If anyone was brave enough to protest, Faiyaz and his gang would create a ruckus at the hotel, ransack the furniture and beat up the patrons. No hotel owner was willing to take the risk to confront him even as he escalated the bulk purchase prices of raw meat. The squint-eyed lout, who had a penchant for leather jackets, gained notoriety with each passing day. His hold on the poultry business was so strong that he came to be known as Koli Faiyaz or Murgi Faiyaz, a moniker that remained with him till his death.

But Koli Faiyaz limited his show of strength to Shivajinagar. His business within the area was flourishing so well that he hardly felt the need to venture out and collect mamool. He had protection from Kotwal but never needed the don's help to function. His minions, from time to time, spread the tales of their dreaded boss across the city. For a long time, Koli Faiyaz's criminal trajectory hovered over half-murders, which in underworld parlance meant a charge of Section 307 (attempt to murder) of the Indian Penal Code (IPC), assault and threatening cases. For him, his business model was extremely profitable. On days when Koli Faiyaz was pleasantly drunk, he would tell his gang members that he was content to just breaking bones and not take anyone's life.

The police turned a blind eye to this menace. Many thought Koli Faiyaz's lavish mutton biryani treats were doing the trick for the men in khaki. What no one knew was that Koli Faiyaz was also an occasional police informer. He had a very strong network through which he knew every activity taking place in Shivajinagar as well as in the rest of Bengaluru. He remained in the good books of many top officers by helping them nab pickpockets, drug dealers, robbers and other criminals. In exchange, the police looked the other way as he monopolized the poultry supply chain.

Koli Faiyaz's clout had grown so much that no one dared to refuse his demands. Once when he learnt of a film shooting that was under way at a hotel in the city, he demanded to be cast in the film. His gang members pulled every string to get him a blink-and-miss role in the movie *Aag Ka Dariya* starring superstar Dilip Kumar. While the film never saw the light of day in Koli Faiyaz's lifetime, he nevertheless enjoyed his stint in Bollywood. He cherished being photographed with Dilip Kumar and actors like Raj Babbar and Shatrughan Sinha who had visited the sets.

Koli Faiyaz's personality was a paradox in itself. Outside home, his one look would be enough to send shivers down people, but at home, he was extremely soft-spoken. He would often wake up startled after watching horror movies, something other gangsters made fun of. Besides flaunting his photographs with movie stars, Koli Faiyaz also bragged about his connection with Haji Mastan, the well-known smuggler from Mumbai. Mastan was said to have a large bungalow in Bengaluru. Whenever he was in the city, Mastan would invite Koli Faiyaz over for drinks.

Koli Faiyaz's family was now living a comfortable life. From working in a poultry shop, he had gone on to open three shops of his own in Russell Market—Faiyaz Poultry Centre, Imtiyaz Poultry Centre and Altaf Poultry Centre, the latter two run by his siblings. Their supply network now extended to Goa and the Maldives. No one dared to break his monopoly in the meat business. Additional income flowed in from the mamool his minions collected from shady lodges and matkas in the area.

Koli Faiyaz's notoriety quotient skyrocketed overnight when he half-murdered Razor Lateef, a rowdy who fiddled with the functioning of his gang. Lateef was known for the swiftness with which he attacked people, using a sharp razor. People who have seen him wielding the blade say he magically swayed it in the air like someone professionally trained in razor fights. When Koli Faiyaz attacked Lateef brutally, it cemented his position as the only Muslim don.

Lateef was a part of Barkat Pehelwan's group, another gang in the area. Barkat Pehelwan hated Koli Faiyaz for the fan following that he enjoyed. Barkat Pehelwan's gang comprising Bashir, Razor Lateef, Chikna Babu and Karate Kamaal were preparing to attack Koli Faiyaz but he somehow got wind of it. Before they could strike, Koli Faiyaz was prepared with his moves. He summoned his trusted lieutenant Tanveer and other members of his gang—Goru, Mysore Road Kalu and Anda Zakir. He treated them to a feast of delicacies, mutton biryani, kebabs and alcohol. Post-midnight, armed with choppers and machetes, Koli Faiyaz and his gang headed to Nova Street where Lateef lived. Koli Faiyaz knocked on the door pretending to be a police inspector.

'*Lateef hain kya?* Police (Is Lateef at home? We're the police),' he asked in his loud voice.

Lateef's unsuspecting mother opened the door and Koli Faiyaz barged in and stabbed Lateef who was lying on his bed. The gang members guarded the door as a blood-soaked Koli Faiyaz emerged from the room with his bloodied machete. The following morning, the police registered a case under Section 307 of the IPC. Lateef had survived after all. The police were now trailing Koli Faiyaz and his gang as Lateef had identified and named each one of them in his statement. Koli Faiyaz who was friends with Mastan and had some other acquaintances in Mumbai fled there for a few weeks before returning to Bengaluru to surrender. Staying away from Bengaluru would lead to huge losses in his meat business, which he had so painstakingly built.

10

Amitabh Bachchan Made Me a Don

The Amitabh Bachchan-starrer *Inquilaab* released in theatres across India in 1984. Excited about watching his favourite actor on the big screen, romancing the then reigning starlet Sridevi, twenty-two-year-old Tanveer Ahmed rushed to Naga Theatre in Shivajinagar. The serpentine queue at the ticket counter made him restless. He broke the queue hoodwinking others and soon got into an argument that took an ugly turn. Tanveer, who was armed with a sharp knife, stabbed one of his attackers in the heat of the moment. As blood splattered from the man's arm, Tanveer fled and took shelter with his guru Koli Faiyaz. This was the first official criminal case registered against Tanveer, a die-hard Bachchan fan who roamed around the lanes of Shivajinagar wearing bell-bottoms that his matinee idol had so popularized.

Born in 1962 at Poor House Hospital in Bengaluru, Tanveer was one of the nine children of Abdul Rauf, a tailor. Rauf shifted with his family to Mumbai's Madanpura, hoping to make more money in the financial capital. But a few years later, Rauf returned to Bengaluru when he found a small shop on Commercial Street for sale at Rs 14,000. He shifted back, family in tow, to Bengaluru in 1973 and rented a modest accommodation near Baitul Mahal Circle in Shivajinagar.

Tanveer, like many youngsters in the neighbourhood, loathed academics. On the pretext of going to school, he'd hang around in shady alleys of Shivajinagar, observing groups of men collecting money from shopkeepers. He would then follow them to their dens where food, drinks and card games were a common affair. Tanveer also began investing time at the Shivajinagar garadis. It is here that he first met local don Koli Faiyaz during an evening workout in the mud pit. Tanveer's elder brothers got wind of his activities and he received a sound thrashing for having bunked school. It was then that Tanveer committed his first theft—an alarm clock that he sold in the market for Rs 22. He used the money to buy a ticket for Rs 14 to Mumbai on Mahalaxmi Express and left for his sister's house in Madanpura. His trip, however, was a short one as his sister made a trunk call informing his elder brothers, who soon came to fetch him. Tanveer, adamant this time, returned home on one condition. 'No one will bash me up,' he warned his elder siblings.

Tanveer could not keep pace with school and began bunking classes again, before giving up studies altogether in Class IX. A well-built teenager now, he started mingling with those in touch with Chudi Pehelwan, a local gangster with a steady extortion business, who also controlled all the garadis in Shivajinagar. Chudi Pehelwan introduced Tanveer to Koli Faiyaz who assigned him petty tasks. During the time, Amitabh Bachchan reigned over the film industry with back-to-back super-hit releases. He had been bestowed with the title 'angry young man' and youngsters aspired to talk, walk and look like him. Tanveer, who had become a fan after watching *Don*, *Muqaddar Ka Sikandar*, *Trishul* and *Mr Natwarlal*, was equally smitten by the actor.

'*Main Amitabh ka aashiq hoon* (I am an Amitabh lover),' he would often tell his friends.

Tanveer was particularly fascinated by Bachchan's style of brandishing a gun or a knife on screen. Back then, Bengaluru was unfamiliar with the gun culture. Knives, choppers, machetes and swords that outlaws referred to as *lambiwali* were more common. Tanveer copied Bachchan's fight sequences and began wielding his chopper in true filmy style.

'*Main jo bhi bana, sirf Bachchan saab ke wajah se bana.* (I owe everything to Bachchan. Whatever I am today is because of him).' That's how Tanveer would often justify his maverick ways with family and friends.

Tanveer's life was a constant cat-and-mouse game because he was forever on the run. He had established himself as one of the most slippery rowdies in the city. The more he was chased, the better he got at escaping from the police's clutches. In 1986, two years after the first case was registered against Tanveer, a rowdy sheet was opened in his name. The rowdy sheet, a booklet compiling the minutest details of notorious criminals, is a mandate followed by the Karnataka Police that contains contact details, hand- and foot-prints, particulars of cases and police stations, modus operandi, among other things. Nowadays, a rowdy sheet also contains email addresses, details of Facebook accounts and other social media pages of the accused. The sheet is created at the discretion of an assistant commissioner of police after he agrees that the rowdy has surpassed a certain level of notoriety. And this sheet is closed only after a deputy commissioner of police (DCP) approves it.

Tanveer's main job was to threaten the local businessmen in the many markets of Shivajinagar on behalf of Koli Faiyaz and gather information on other goons who conspired against his boss. By the time Tanveer turned twenty-four, he had ten cases registered against him, including that of an attempt to murder, theft, threat and extortion. He once beat up a tea-shop owner savagely simply because he learnt that the owner did not approve of Koli Faiyaz's way of conducting business. In another case, an extortionist named Fruit Razzak, who collected mamool from fruit vendors in the area, could not accept the growing popularity of Koli Faiyaz and ordered his hit. Koli Faiyaz was attacked suddenly and he sustained severe injuries. He spent the next seven months recovering from the wounds caused by swords and machetes. As soon as he was back on his feet, he decided to seek revenge from Fruit Razzak, and Tanveer was tasked to head the operation. The revenge drama led to seven half-murders.

After the brutal attack on Razor Lateef at his residence, Tanveer accompanied Koli Faiyaz to Mumbai. They initially took shelter in a dense slum pocket called Bandra Plot in the suburb of Jogeshwari. But within seven months, money started drying up and Koli Faiyaz decided to return to Bengaluru where his earnings came from, and surrendered to the police. Koli Faiyaz sent his punters, including Tanveer, to another contact in Nagpada, a Muslim-dominated area in Mumbai. This is where Tanveer first met the men who worked for Dawood Ibrahim.

Dawood Ibrahim had left Indian shores but one of his relatives had an office called Shams Travels in Mumbai's Temkar mohalla. His chief lieutenant Chhota Shakeel and another punter, Ejaz Pathan, who was later convicted in the 1993 serial blasts in Mumbai, were often seen at the Shams office. Tanveer joined them in carrying out errands, fetching chai and *paani* for the high-profile visitors at the office. It was the first time Tanveer had seen actors, singers and cricketers up-close and was thrilled by the access that his job had earned him.

The short tryst with the Mumbai underworld had left Tanveer hungry for more. But his elder brothers squashed his plans and sent him off to Saudi Arabia to work and escape the police.

When Tanveer returned a few months later, his family, tired of daily police visits, pleaded with him to surrender. He went and handed himself over at

KG Halli Police Station. After his arrest, Tanveer was sent to Bengaluru Central Jail, where he first came in contact with the gang members of Oil Kumar. He met Agrahara Bachchan, Mani Bharti, Krishnaji Rao alias Kitty, Renuka Acharya alias Kariya, Pushparaj alias Pushpa alias Lotus, Bekinnakannu Rajendra or 'cat-eyed Rajendra' and Tamti Sanjeeva. He knew that they had earlier owed allegiance to Jayaraj but something seemed to have changed and now they regarded Oil Kumar as their boss. They had all heard of Tanveer, who had earned the reputation of being one of the most slippery rowdies. They approached him for a conversation, something Tanveer took pride in.

Tanveer observed how all these men had hush-hush conversations and regular group meetings. It seemed something big was being planned. He would notice the men having intense discussions during lunch and dinner breaks with Kitty leading the talks. The animated conversations included the mention of using a gun, something that Tanveer had never heard of before. The conversations intrigued him and he tried to be friendlier with the men. He would narrate stories of how he evaded the police and entertained them with jokes. His most popular story was when he was hiding in a shanty in a farm with a few of his aides and the police closed in on them. Tanveer ran for his life wearing nothing but his underpants only to bang into a wall that came crumbling down on him. Luckily, he fell into a pit and evaded arrest once again. The next morning, he emerged from the hole draped in a gunny bag. Everyone had a hearty laugh every time he relayed this story.

After several weeks, the men let their guard down in Tanveer's presence and he finally got to know what was being planned: the assassination of Jayaraj.

11

Bhugataloka Gets Bloodthirsty

The Kanishka attack reverberated through the underworld for the reckless flouting of the unwritten rules of mafiadom. Kotwal had broken all of them and was now looked upon as an untrustworthy backstabber.

Jayaraj employed all his resources to ensure that Kotwal was arrested for attempting to murder him. But the slippery Kotwal gave the police a good run. The cops had begun to interrogate all those who knew or had worked with Kotwal at some point. Suddenly, no one wanted to flaunt their connection with the deadly don. An anti-rowdy squad was formed to track down Kotwal at any cost.

This was not the first time that the police were under pressure to nab Kotwal. Back in 1983, the brazen criminal had dared to barge into the highly secured Vidhana Soudha, the seat of the state legislature, to threaten the then chief minister Ramakrishna Hegde. Kotwal was a supporter of S. Bangarappa and even carried out tasks for him. When Bangarappa's dream of becoming the chief minister was squashed with Hegde's appointment, Kotwal flew into a rage. He entered the heavily guarded area and barged into Hegde's cabin demanding that he step down and make way for Bangarappa. He did not stop there. He even threatened Hegde's daughter to mount pressure on her father. Needless to say, the fuming chief minister put the entire police force at work to nab Kotwal. Even then, an anti-rowdy squad was formed but to no avail. There were sixteen warrants in Kotwal's name and the police were yet to trace him.

* * *

As swords and machetes splattered blood on Bengaluru's streets, a love story blossomed on the sidelines. Varadaraj Nayak, the son of a wealthy businessman, fell in love with a middle-class girl. But soon their love story turned sour over class differences. Varada's father had a flourishing business of manufacturing almond premix. He couldn't stomach the fact that his son was in love with a girl from a lower socio-economic background.

Nowadays, young couples go to expensive restaurants, malls, discotheques and coffee shops on dates. However, back in the 1980s, it was Bengaluru's many gardens that proved to be the perfect hideouts for couples seeking quiet spots far from the madding crowd. From Cubbon Park in the centre of the city, to Lalbagh in south Bengaluru, the thick foliage offered shade and cover to many couples. Varada and his girlfriend spent hours in these parks planning their future together. They walked for hours on end, arms locked, along the city's beautiful lakes, never wanting the moment to end. But their bliss was short-lived. One night after Varada dropped his girlfriend home, she was accosted by six well-built men on motorcycles. They circled her till she screamed in fear.

'Stop meeting Varada. End your relationship with him or we will kill you and your family,' one of the men threatened her. 'Do you want your pretty face to be ruined with acid?'

The men sported thick gold chains with tiger-nail pendants and yellow metal watches. They pulled out their knives and machetes and pointed them at her. The girl stood petrified on the road, covered in cold sweat, her voice caught in her throat. Then she ran into her house, trying to fight the darkness in front of her eyes. She grabbed the telephone and dialled Varada's number and told him about her ordeal. It turned out that Varada's father had sought help from some local strongmen, who in turn had passed on the job to Kotwal.

In his free time, Varada would hang out with rookie rowdies in the area. When he sought their help in this matter, they introduced him to Bachchan and Sreedhar. Varada pleaded the duo to ward off Kotwal's men.

'I can't live without her. We need to find a way out of this,' Varada begged after telling them the whole story.

Sreedhar and Bachchan had become close friends and carried out almost all their tasks together. They had a steady source of income thanks to several small assignments coming their way. But after the Kanishka attack, Bachchan's name had cropped up in the police investigation, forcing the duo to go underground. They hopped from one guest house to another, changing their hideouts every week. But Varada always found ways to reach them. They would discuss how to get back at Kotwal for hours. The trio eventually worked out a plan—Varada would seek help from Kotwal and try to get the don on his side. Sreedhar would play the conduit and get closer to Kotwal.

In February 1986, Bengaluru was a hotbed of political action. Hegde had put in his resignation after the court held his Janata Party government's act of awarding several arrack-bottling contracts as unlawful. The cops were busy with bandobast for the heavy political activity that was brewing in the government headquarters of Karnataka. Sreedhar seized this opportunity to track down Kotwal and arrange a meeting to put forward Varada's case. To his amusement, Kotwal was found in the most unexpected way possible.

Kotwal, who was on the run, knew that Jayaraj's men were baying for his blood. He and his right-hand man, Seetharam Shetty, stayed away from Bengaluru and took shelter in and around Tumkur. Not too far from the city, Tumkur was known for its rich coconut and areca-nut plantations. The duo made quick visits to the city on their motorcycle to gauge the scenario and get updates. As it so happened, Sreedhar and Bachchan too were hiding in lodges near Tumkur, trying to avoid any run-ins with the police. One night, when Sreedhar, Bachchan and

Varada were together, they suddenly heard a motorcycle approaching in the dark. It was Kotwal and Seetharam, who stopped the bike on spotting the trio. What Kotwal asked them next startled the three men.

'Do you know of any safe place to hide in for a few days?' Kotwal asked.

They found it comical that the man whom they had been trying to hunt down had almost offered himself on a platter. Sreedhar, who didn't miss the vulnerability in the don's voice, quickly suggested that all of them head to a nearby farmhouse owned by a man called Ninge Gowda. Tired of being on the run, Kotwal agreed without sensing any foul play.

It was a sprawling house amid sugarcane plantations with hardly any living soul around. Kotwal thought it was the perfect hideout. He spent hours sitting on the porch while the others played cards. A young boy named Kitty, who had grown up hearing stories of Kotwal, was the only outsider in the farmhouse. He would do odd jobs like cleaning, fetching food and running errands for the guests. On days Kotwal went out with Seetharam on his motorcycle, which was once every three to four days, Kitty would ensure that there was no danger lurking around. A few days later, one of Kotwal's two wives joined him.

One day, when Kotwal planned to visit Bengaluru to review the situation, he asked Sreedhar to join him. Sreedhar promptly hopped on to the Rajdoot Yamaha. They made a pit stop at a telephone booth from where Kotwal made a few calls. The two entered Bengaluru wearing monkey caps to hide their faces. Kotwal's next stop was at a brothel. Sreedhar stood guard at the entrance as Kotwal spent time inside. His next destination was his house in Indiranagar where some of his gang members were waiting for him. He inquired if any cops had come looking for him. His final stop was at an oil pump where he met a man and left a message for Oil Kumar, asking for a meeting. Kotwal knew very well that Oil Kumar had good connections, who could help bail him out of his present situation.

Unaware that a dramatic chase awaited them, the duo began their return journey to Tumkur. As Kotwal approached the Kanteerava Stadium, a chill ran down his spine. Even Sreedhar sensed the fear that had suddenly gripped Kotwal. A few metres ahead was Inspector B.K. Shivaram on his Bullet with a constable riding pillion. And as it so happened, Shivaram too spotted Kotwal, identifying him instantly. Panic-stricken, Kotwal started speeding but Shivaram closed in on him. A part of the anti-rowdy squad formed to nab Kotwal, Shivaram was among the few men who could identify the Robbery King and Sreedhar at a glance.

When Shivaram almost caught up with them, he ordered the constable to train his gun on Kotwal and Sreedhar. He told him to shoot at least one round in the air to scare Kotwal so that he surrendered. But the constable, who had never fired a gun in his career, developed cold feet. Seeing his prey getting away, Shivaram tried to kick Kotwal's motorcycle. However, Kotwal swerved his bike and managed to escape, leaving Shivaram fuming.

Mune Gowda

One of the many garadi manes
in Bengaluru that are now on
the verge of extinction.

Kotwal Ramchandra

M.P. Jayaraj at a garadi mane.

Jayaraj (right) with Rajiv Gandhi.

Jayaraj at an election rally.

Jayaraj (right) with his supporters.

Jayaraj (second from left) in a meeting of All India Small and Medium Newspapers Federation.

An edition of *Garibi Hatavo*. The headline reads: 'An Open Letter to Dr Rajkumar from Jayaraj'.

Another edition of the same newspaper. The headline reads: 'Chief Minister Hegde's Letter'.

Jayaraj (bottom left) at an event.

Jayaraj at a function in Bengaluru.

Jayaraj with his family.

Jayaraj's body was kept at his Wilson Garden residence for public viewing.

Hotel Kanishka. Jayaraj was attacked here by Kotwal Ramchandra and his gang on 3 January 1986.

Rowdy N. Shekhar, who was killed in Bengaluru Police's first-ever encounter.

Shiva Kumar, alias
Oil Kumar

Faiyaz Ahmed, alias
Koli Faiyaz

Tanveer

Faiyaz Ahmed with Dilip Kumar. He had a blink-and-
miss role in the movie *Aag Ka Dariya*.

Faiyaz Ahmed with Raj Babbar and Shatrughan Sinha
on the sets of *Aag Ka Dariya*.

Agni Sreedhar

An old photograph of Rai in the police records.

Rai unwinding on a holiday.

A handcuffed Rai being brought back to
Bengaluru from Dubai.

Courtesy of S.K. Umesh

Muthappa Rai

Courtesy of Muthappa Rai

Courtesy of Muthappa Rai official page

Rai poses with a broom during a
cleanliness drive at Kalasipalyam
market, Bengaluru.

Courtesy of Muthappa Rai fan page

Rai waves at a crowd of followers
as he leaves an event.

Courtesy of Jaya Karnataka official page

Rai beside his Land Cruiser.

Rai with actor Vivek Oberoi. Oberoi is reportedly slated to play Rai in an upcoming biopic on the gangster directed by Ram Gopal Varma.

Rai at his son Ricky's wedding reception.

Two signages prohibiting guests from carrying arms and clicking photographs during the reception.

The close shave had left Sreedhar and Kotwal shaken. They knew Shivaram would've pulled the trigger if he had the gun in his own hands. When the duo reached Tumkur, the calm environs of the farmhouse slowed down their racing hearts. They spent the night narrating the day's events to Bachchan, Varada and Seetharam.

The farmhouse was becoming a rather comfortable refuge for Kotwal when Sreedhar started thinking about how close he was to attacking the Robbery King. With the help of Bachchan and Varada, he could easily kill him and the police would only be thankful to them for doing so. But Sreedhar was also wary of being implicated in a murder. At times when Kotwal and Seetharam were busy, the trio discussed how and when they could attack the don. But they continued to delay their plan. Sreedhar decided to approach Jayaraj and make him an offer he couldn't refuse.

'I will get Kotwal killed. In return, I want complete immunity. I don't want a murder charge on me and I don't want to go to jail,' Sreedhar said. 'I also want Bachchan and Varada to be protected.'

Jayaraj could not refuse such an offer even though he was doubtful of Sreedhar and his men bringing down Kotwal. He assured Sreedhar that he would take complete responsibility for the murder.

It was strange how Kotwal, a man who never let his guard down and was usually suspicious of everyone around him, remained completely oblivious to the murder plan being hatched right under his nose. Not once did the thought cross his mind that he was living under the same roof as his killers. But his trusted aide Seetharam knew something was cooking. He tried his best to gain the confidence of Sreedhar's gang but nothing worked till he approached the trio one day and said something that turned their heads.

'Let's kill him,' Seetharam said.

Sreedhar, Bachchan and Varada looked at each other in shock. Why would Seetharam want to kill Kotwal? They stared at him in disbelief but his gaze was unflinching.

'He is a maniac. I have seen his ugliest side. If ever he has to kill me to save his own neck, he will do so without batting an eyelid,' Seetharam reasoned.

Seetharam had grown up the hard way, working in small eateries in Bengaluru since childhood. As he grew up, he joined a pro-Kannada organization where rogue elements found support under the garb of activism. Seetharam was known for his hot temperament as any difference of opinion with him would often result in fights. His clashes with rowdy Bekinnakannu Rajendra, were well known. It was Kotwal who came across Seetharam and offered him a place in his gang. Seetharam remained loyal and went on to become Kotwal's right-hand man. One order from Kotwal and Seetharam would get things done. But despite so many years of service, Seetharam could never get one thing from his master—respect.

'He treats me like dirt. I have given him so many years but he treats me like my existence doesn't matter,' Seetharam said.

From three, it was now four against one. Kotwal stood alone. He was so focused on the danger outside that he had completely missed what was churning in his own backyard. When Kotwal was not around, the four would gather to discuss the execution step by step. But every time their plans would come to naught at one point. Kotwal never went to sleep until he was sure that everyone else was asleep.

However, one night, Seetharam heard someone snoring loudly in a hut in the compound of the house. He immediately knew that his boss was catching up on his lost sleep. It was the night of 22 March 1986.

After dinner that night, Kotwal had headed to a dingy hut in the compound. Everyone had assumed that he would be wide awake as always staring at the roof till they heard him snoring. He was in deep sleep, perhaps he had finally let go of the fear that he had been harbouring all those days. Seetharam peeked inside the hut and then rushed out to inform the others. Sreedhar, Bachchan and Varada were smoking. Kotwal did not allow them to smoke around him.

'He has dozed off. It's time. Let's get it done,' Seetharam said breathlessly.

They looked at each other and without exchanging any words, rushed to get their weapons. Varada did not carry any weapon. Sreedhar picked up his nunchaku. Sreedhar wondered if he was still vindictive. He felt nothing inside but went along with the plan anyway. He thought his predicament was similar to that of the Vicario brothers' in the novella *Chronicle of a Death*

Foretold written by Gabriel Garcia Marquez. His resolve to avenge the attack on his brother way back in 1979 had weakened and somewhere in his heart, he even wanted to avoid the killing. But the situation he was in called for the job to be done.

The men tiptoed inside the hut and circled Kotwal. They looked at each other for a final nod. And then hacked him to death. There was no revolt, no struggle. It was the easiest killing the underworld had ever known of. A sudden silence descended over the farmhouse. Sreedhar, Bachchan and Varada lit cigarettes and began smoking while Seetharam sat next to Kotwal's body and wept inconsolably. It was hard to understand what was going on in his mind but when they had attacked, it was Seetharam who had dealt the most brutal and the fatal blows. The others had only struck feeble blows.

Seetharam continued to howl and began cleaning up the blood-splattered room. They were worried that Kitty might arrive at any moment to ensure that Kotwal was safe. Kitty was an ardent fan of Kotwal's and if anyone could rat them out, it would be him.

Meanwhile, in Bengaluru, the manhunt for Kotwal was getting intense. Shivaram was consumed with anger after he failed to nab Kotwal despite being within arm's reach. He had taken it upon himself to hunt him down. Kotwal's relatives and gang members were harassed so much by the police interrogations that they announced that they had severed all ties with the don. On the few occasions when they did that, Kotwal called them up and threatened them. Suddenly his threat calls had stopped. Shivaram too stopped receiving tip-offs about his movements. He started growing suspicious.

Back in Tumkur, Sreedhar, Bachchan and Seetharam dug up a small pit inside the compound and buried Kotwal's body for the time being. Before the burial, Bachchan put some marks on the body for identification and also planted a tiny sapling on the spot. Jayaraj refused to believe them till he saw the body himself. Nevertheless, he was ecstatic. Despite his disbelief, Jayaraj paid a token amount of Rs 5000 to Sreedhar and Bachchan and sent two of his men to fetch the body. Wary after the Kanishka attack, Jayaraj suspected that it could be another sinister plan hatched by Kotwal to kill him. So he readied a group of over one hundred men and asked them to be on standby. What if Sreedhar and Bachchan were fooling him and leading him into a bigger trap?

Jayaraj's doubts were soon dispelled. He received a trunk call from the two men he had sent along with Sreedhar.

'Anna, it's him. One hundred per cent!'

Jayaraj ordered them to bring the body. They dug it out, stuffed it in the boot of an Ambassador and brought it to Jayaraj. He went into a fit of euphoria when he saw Kotwal lying lifeless in front of him. He spat on the body several times, mouthing expletives. For a moment, he forgot that Kotwal was dead and bragged to the body with the pride of a triumphant man. He was so consumed with his victory that he decided to hang the body at the entrance of Vidhana Soudha to make a statement. But when he called up his lawyers, each one of them rejected his plan. They convinced him to cremate Kotwal's body so that nothing could be traced back to him.

Jayaraj sent a few of his gang members to take the body to a remote village on the border of Karnataka. According to the legal advice he received, he ordered the body to be burnt.

When Jayaraj informed his lawyers that the job was done, he got a firing again.

'How could they have left the charred body on the spot? Clean it up completely and throw the ashes in the sea. Not a particle should be left behind,' one of his lawyers told him.

Jayaraj ordered three of his men to clear up the dry well where Kotwal's charred remains had been disposed of. He paid them Rs 10,000 and asked them to go to Madras to throw the remains in the sea.

* * *

Shivaram was having sleepless nights. He could not get over the image of Kotwal speeding on his motorcycle and Sreedhar turning around at regular intervals to check how close he had got to them. That Kotwal was probably dead was also discussed in hush-hush tones among the rowdies. But no one could say anything with certainty. Besides Kotwal, Shivaram had put Sreedhar, Bachchan and Seetharam on the target list. He knew that one of these three would lead him to Kotwal. Another thing that had struck Shivaram was a sudden change in Jayaraj's confidence. He had started coming out in the open more often and his daytime movements had also increased considerably. It definitely meant something, Shivaram thought. On the other hand, he also got several reports of Sreedhar, Bachchan and Seetharam being spotted on a bike. The police had nicknamed them 'one, two, three' as they would often be spotted triple-riding on one motorcycle. But there was no news of Kotwal.

In June 1986, almost three months after Kotwal's murder, Shivaram and his team finally managed to trace Seetharam, who was holed up in his village in Udupi district. The police team was disappointed that Kotwal was not with him but nonetheless it was a good lead. Within a day of the police 'treatment' in the lockup, Seetharam began to sing. He narrated everything that had happened.

The police cracked down on thirteen people and eventually arrested Jayaraj as well. Jayaraj had accepted without qualms that he was behind Kotwal's murder and was now the undisputed don of Bengaluru. Kotwal's gang members were slowly siding with Jayaraj. The police started zeroing in on Sreedhar, Bachchan and Varada and they finally nabbed the trio five months after Kotwal's death. But despite so many arrests, they couldn't substantiate their charges till the body was found.

After several days of inflicting torture on the arrested rowdies, the cops finally got lucky. Everyone, including Jayaraj, was under the impression that Kotwal's remains were now in the sea. But his three minions, who had been assigned the job, had faltered. On the promise of being made police witnesses and thus getting lesser punishments, they confessed to Shivaram that Kotwal's remains were actually in a well on the outskirts of Bengaluru. It turned out that the trio had decided to split the money that Jayaraj had given them to travel to Madras, and disposed of the remains in a nearby well and informed Jayaraj two days later that the job was done.

Shivaram and his team rushed to the spot. The well was filled with water to the brim. A local contractor was called to pump out the water. The task took eleven hours. Eventually, a gunny bag was pulled out of the well in which the police found small pieces of bones and teeth. For Shivaram and his team, the remains were more valuable than diamonds.

The remains were sent to the Forensic Science Laboratory in Madras where the forensic examination was carried out by the same doctor who years later would examine the remains of Prime Minister Rajiv Gandhi after his assassination in 1991.

With Kotwal's murder and Jayaraj's arrest, there was an eerie calm in Bengaluru's underworld. Oil Kumar was worried about his fate. Sreedhar and Bachchan gained notoriety with Kotwal's murder. But for the cops, they continued to be *chindis* (inconsequential) as Shivaram would often refer to them. For them, Kotwal and Jayaraj were the most daring rowdies and no one else ever matched up to them in Bengaluru. While Sreedhar's importance had grown, the cops circulated stories of how he had not even touched Kotwal's body.

'Sreedhar did not even look at it. He was simply present in the room at the time of the killing,' was Shivaram's version. There was only one thing that was discussed in the underworld—Kotwal's murder. The gangsters said he was 'backstabbed'. They labelled Sreedhar, Bachchan and Seetharam as traitors. After all, Kotwal had trusted them and they had killed him in his sleep. For the criminals, these men were a treacherous bunch in the crime world.

12

The Rise of the Maharaja

History has it that a ruler rules best from the capital of his kingdom, the epicentre of his power. But Jayaraj was different. He remained incarcerated for many years and yet managed to call the shots from the confines of his prison cell. Being behind bars did not affect Jayaraj. He enjoyed freedom like no one else did.

A few days after his arrest in the Kotwal murder case, Jayaraj got himself admitted to the jail ward of Victoria Hospital. He also managed to get Sreedhar and Bachchan moved to the hospital so that they could keep him company. The rest of his gang members too had access to them at any time of the day or night. One of the regular visitors was Oil Kumar, who came with Jayaraj's share of protection money and updates on his businesses. But despite his proximity to Jayaraj, Oil Kumar was living under the constant fear of being killed and disposed of in the dead of night, a fate Kotwal had met. Oil Kumar knew the gangster wouldn't spare his life either, if he ever got wind of the fact that he was the mastermind behind the Kanishka attack. Before Jayaraj's arrest, Oil Kumar landed at his house with his wife Rita. The couple fell at Jayaraj's feet pleading for forgiveness. Jayaraj grew mad with rage when he found out about the plan; he could not even bring himself to look at Oil Kumar but he did not like that a woman was crying at his feet. The melodramatic plan had worked out after all. Jayaraj assured them that he would forgive Oil Kumar's role in the Kanishka attack. However, a seed of doubt had taken root inside Jayaraj's mind. He knew Oil Kumar was not trustworthy and had to be eliminated.

Jayaraj would step outside the jail ward once a week. A taxi would be called for him and along with a police escort he would enjoy his day, visit a bar and his house and then head back to the ward. He would often coax Sreedhar to come along with him and have fun. But Sreedhar would politely refuse except on occasions he visited Gangaram Book Store on MG Road. He bought books worth a few thousand rupees, which sufficed him for at least a year. The few hours of freedom felt like bliss to him.

In the corridors of the government-run hospital, Jayaraj would stroll for hours in the mornings and in the evenings with Sreedhar in tow. Jayaraj enjoyed the conversations with Sreedhar—on the one hand, Sreedhar enjoyed the thrill of the crime world and its dangers, on the other hand, he wanted to live like any other law-abiding youth in Bengaluru. It was this tussle that Jayaraj enjoyed the most. He often thought that his fight was similar to that of Sreedhar's. He too wanted a dignified image and used the tag of being the editor of a newspaper to that end. Jayaraj had a plan. He eventually wanted to shed the image of a crime lord and adopt a more respectable one. During one of his group meetings in the hospital ward, he proudly announced that he would venture into a business that was completely legal.

'I don't want to be talked about in the crime world for too long. Maybe a year or two, at the most. After that I will join the white-collar brigade,' the Maharaja spelt out his future.

Jayaraj had always thought of himself as a philanthropic man. Those who worked with him also say that he had a soft corner for the poor and the needy. Once, during his morning stroll, he saw a woman weeping in the hospital corridor. He summoned Sreedhar and asked him to find out what was wrong. Sreedhar promptly reported back.

'The woman has lost her husband. She has no money to clear the bill and take his body for the last rites to their village on the outskirts of Bengaluru.'

All she needed was Rs 500. But Jayaraj handed Rs 2000 to Sreedhar and asked him to give the money to the grieving woman.

'It's almost forty years since Independence and people are still struggling for such basic needs. Sreedhar, always do something for the poor,' Jayaraj said, walking away after patting Sreedhar on the shoulder. The latter was touched by the gesture.

Sreedhar thought, 'This man has a heart of gold.'

* * *

On 18 August 1987, a lawyer named Abdul Rasheed was found dead on the railway tracks in Salem, Tamil Nadu. A native of Kerala, Rasheed was representing P. Sadashivan, the founder of the Visvesvaraya Trust, which was set up with the prime objective of starting a medical college in Kolar, Karnataka. It later turned out that the Ramkrishna Hegde government in power had decided to substitute Sadashivan's trust with the Devaraj Urs Trust run by Home Minister R.L. Jalappa.

Rasheed had come to Bengaluru to carry out some paperwork related to the case just four days before his death. He had visited Sanjay Gandhi College of Education on Millers Road located in the jurisdiction of the High Grounds Police Station and under K. Narayan, DCP (west). He was allegedly roughed up by the police during his visit to the college and taken to the High Grounds Police Station on charges of misbehaving with the principal of the college, Rathna. Rasheed was booked and presented before a metropolitan magistrate, where he told the court that he was a lawyer and was being framed and tortured by the police. He begged to be released on bail. The magistrate granted him bail after which he went back to Sandhya Lodge on Subedar Chatram Road where he was staying. The next day, Rasheed sent out a strongly worded letter to the press stating that the police and the home minister were after his life. He also sent a letter to the Bar Association highlighting the threat to his life. He disappeared soon after.

On 18 August, Rasheed's badly injured body was discovered by a railway gang man on the tracks in Salem, about 200 kilometres from Bengaluru. His body was identified by his brother. The key of a room at Sandhya Lodge found in his pocket led the police to the place where he was staying in Bengaluru. His death raised a furore in the legal fraternity. The investigation was initially handled by the Corps of Detectives, an elite investigation agency of the Karnataka Police. But after a protest led by lawyers, the government gave in and transferred the case to the Central Bureau of Investigation (CBI).

A few lawyers approached Jayaraj, who was still in jail at that time, for support. Jayaraj realized it was a fight against the police and agreed to help without a second thought. He offered his full support to the lawyers and fuelled their anger by calling regular meetings in the jail ward and instigating them. Sreedhar warned Jayaraj to not go against the police with all guns blazing. The police and the home minister were involved in the case and Sreedhar felt it might backfire on Jayaraj. But Jayaraj remained adamant and ignored his advice.

'This is the only way to take control and rise,' Jayaraj reasoned with Sreedhar, who thought that Rasheed's murder would have gone unnoticed had it not been for Jayaraj's involvement. He began to think it was the beginning of Jayaraj's end.

With Jayaraj's backing, the lawyers agitated with great vigour. They called for strikes, came out on the streets, stopped taking up police cases and openly spoke to the press against the police. It left the government helpless.

The investigations eventually led to the arrest of DCP Narayan and five other policemen. Jalappa too was forced to resign in May 1988.

By this time, Jayaraj had come out of jail with his old ambition of becoming a messiah revived like never before. In the court, Kitty, the sole police witness who could bring the murderers of Kotwal to book, refused to identify any of the accused. After assuring the cops that he would testify against the killers, Kitty had suddenly disappeared. The police suspected that Oil Kumar and Sreedhar's brother, Basanth Kumar, had kidnapped him. Both were picked up by Inspector Shivaram for questioning but they revealed nothing. Kitty reappeared for the next hearing but didn't name any of the accused. All the other witnesses also turned hostile. The court acquitted Jayaraj for lack of evidence. Of the twenty months that Jayaraj was in jail as an undertrial, he had spent thirteen in the hospital's jail ward. Jayaraj's acquittal greatly upset Oil Kumar. He started planning Jayaraj's murder.

Jayaraj wore DCP Narayan's arrest as a badge and his first victory in the fight for social causes. From Victoria Hospital's jail ward, Jayaraj had shifted his meetings with the lawyers to the car shed of his residence near Wilson Garden. Food and alcohol were provided generously. The who's who of the legal community attended these meetings.

There was a simmering anger within the police force. Jayaraj's support to the lawyers was something they could not digest. His blatant attacks on the police through his newspaper further miffed them. Jayaraj used his acquittal in the Kotwal murder case to ridicule the police and brazenly questioned their efficiency in tracking down the killer. His audacity was surprising given that he himself was behind the murder. Jayaraj did not even hesitate to call the police 'killers' and 'corrupt'.

* * *

In the Muslim underworld, Koli Faiyaz continued to rule the roost.

After Kotwal's murder, Koli Faiyaz paid a customary visit to Jayaraj to let the don know that he was now on his side. Koli Faiyaz's power had increased tremendously. He had several offers from rowdies outside Shivajinagar to join hands, but he refused, saying that his business was his priority. He became a dreaded name in the city after he committed his first murder in the year 1988 in broad daylight.

A man named Naem had settled in Bengaluru's Banaswadi after returning from Saudi Arabia. The Bengaluru Police claimed he was one of the very first drug peddlers in the city. Naem smuggled brown sugar, an adulterated form of heroin, and sold it in small quantities to youngsters outside universities. Cops said that his main clientele comprised Iranian students, who had started migrating to the city for studies. The underworld called him 'Saap Naem', a nickname he earned for keeping several snake species as his pets. He was a snake-bite addict and soon started offering it to other addicts at a cost. While Naem started becoming a problem for the Bengaluru cops, he was an eyesore for Koli Faiyaz too. Koli Faiyaz did not approve of the drug business and more importantly, Naem was spreading his wings in Shivajinagar by supplying drugs to youngsters as well as gaining the confidence of shopkeepers who were against Koli Faiyaz.

Naem's thriving business started giving Koli Faiyaz sleepless nights. Such was his insecurity that he had started drinking his imported whisky during the day. The thought that Naem would have a greater clout in Shivajinagar bothered him to no end. His anger and insecurity, combined with alcohol, were becoming a lethal concoction. Every day, he would get complaints about Naem and his minions beating up his gang members. He longed each day for Naem's blood but waited for the right time to strike.

Naem, who was said to be trained in karate, relished every nugget of information on how Koli Faiyaz was getting restless. He found Koli Faiyaz's ethical stand against the drug business almost comical. 'A shameless criminal and extortionist is against drugs. What a fool!'

Naem had illegally taken possession of a house in Frazer Town that belonged to the father of Bollywood actress Neetu Singh, now married to actor Rishi Kapoor. She had worked in blockbusters such as *Deewar, Kabhi Kabhi, Amar Akbar Anthony,* among others. Her father tried everything to get Naem to vacate the house but even the police could not help. The cops finally entrusted Koli Faiyaz with the job, knowing well that the two were rivals. Koli Faiyaz made many attempts to get the house vacated but failed. His restlessness only grew as this task was assigned to him by the cops and his reputation was at stake. Frustrated, he asked his gang members to keep a close watch on Naem.

'As soon as he is vulnerable, I will attack him,' he announced his plan.

It was 1988 and one of the country's biggest hits, *Qayamat Se Qayamat Tak*, starring Aamir Khan and Juhi Chawla, had released to a grand opening. Koli Faiyaz's men spotted Naem and his eight-year-old son watching the film at Lido Theatre on MG Road. They rushed to their boss with the information. Koli Faiyaz picked up a butcher's knife from his shop and took position outside the theatre. As soon as Naem walked out with his son, Koli Faiyaz attacked him. Naem ran for his life towards Ulsoor and entered a hotel's lobby. Koli Faiyaz dragged him out and attacked him fiercely, making multiple deep gashes on Naem's body. Assuming that Naem had died, they dumped the body in a small room in Shivajinagar till Koli Faiyaz decided what was to be done with it. The men didn't know what to do with Naem's son. They finally decided to put him in an autorickshaw and send him home. Later in the night, when one of the gang members went to check on the body, to his utter shock he found that Naem was breathing. But Koli Faiyaz was determined not to give him any chance to survive.

Early in the morning, he dragged out Naem to the Beef Market in Shivajinagar. Koli Faiyaz flexed his muscles and lifted Naem and swirled his body in the air, banging his head on a huge rock. Blood splattered on his face but Koli Faiyaz remained unfazed. Naem died a death that was typical of poultry in Shivajinagar's butcher shops: brutal and ghastly. The sight shocked the people in the area. Koli Faiyaz's terror had reached a new height that day.

But Koli Faiyaz was arrested for murder after Naem's son testified as a witness. He was jailed for more than five years till the high court acquitted him for lack of evidence.

* * *

Back home from jail, Jayaraj spent some quality time with his family. He had only one man to deal with: Oil Kumar. Though he had pleaded for forgiveness, Jayaraj knew that Oil Kumar was a backstabber. But Jayaraj failed to foresee something. That it was not an individual but the entire police force that was baying for his blood now.

13

Tiger Becomes Trigger-Happy

With Jayaraj's clout, everyone associated with him started commanding great influence. At the Bengaluru city railway station in the Majestic area, one such man was N. Shekhar. Shekhar and his father, Acharappa, ran a tourist bus agency called Seagull Travels. With Jayaraj's backing, Shekhar controlled the business coming from tourists who made a stop at Bengaluru to head to travel destinations like Coorg, Mysuru and Ooty. Shekhar and his minions spread terror by beating up coolies and other tourist operators. His modus operandi was simple: the terrorized coolies would take a majority of the tourists to the Seagull Travels' stall even though he charged twice the rate as compared to other agents. The coolies who did not give in to his demands, were beaten up in broad daylight by Shekhar, his accomplice Ganesh alias Kalapatthar and other members of his gang. His competitors maintained a distance and survived on whatever remaining business they could get. His lawless activities in that area even earned him the nickname of 'Station Shekhar'. He was a staunch follower of Jayaraj and paid him decent mamool.

Station Shekhar ensured that Jayaraj's share was never delayed. The business around the railway station was expanding as more vacationers chose to spend time in Karnataka's serene locations. But every now and then, someone would stand up to Station Shekhar's atrocities and disrupt his lawless dealings. A man called Rajendra, who was a rowdy-sheeter from Srirampura, had begun to spread his wings. Station Shekhar got paranoid but he wanted to set an example so that no one ever dared to cross his path again. Things came to a pass one day when Station Shekhar confronted Rajendra. The argument soon escalated into a fist fight. Station Shekhar pulled out a machete and slashed Rajendra's chest, butchering him to death in public view. A crowd had gathered around the railway station but no one dared to intervene, not even the three constables who witnessed the brutal attack. Station Shekhar calmly walked up to a water fountain in the station and washed the blood-stained weapon and himself, halted an autorickshaw and left. He gave enough time for someone to apprehend him but he knew no one had the guts to do so.

The murder in broad daylight made the headlines of every newspaper the next morning, some even went on to report how eyewitnesses had spotted three constables in the crowd. The police sprang into action by registering a case of murder against Station Shekhar, who went underground along with his father. Investigations led to a dead end as no one knew where he lived, and those who did, didn't dare utter a word. A telling sign of the dominance of rowdies in the streets of Bengaluru was their audacity to roam around freely and the police turning a blind eye to their antics. One day, weeks after the murder, Station Shekhar confidently stepped out of his hideout, craving for some entertainment. He and his gang headed to Savera, a live-band restaurant on MG Road. Shekhar made several requests to the alluringly dressed singer to croon his favourite songs. At a distance from Station Shekhar's group, sat the Chhota Pehelwan gang from Shivajinagar. Both gangs were high on spirits. The gang members struggled to put down their requests on chits of paper and pass it on to the singer as was the norm. They started whistling and passing comments at her. When the woman began singing the next song, the Chhota Pehelwan gang was annoyed that it wasn't the one they had requested for. When they learnt that the request had come from Station Shekhar, an argument started, which led to a scuffle. The singer, waitresses and the other patrons began running helter-skelter as a brawl broke out. Savera's owner, Abdullah, rushed to stop the gangs from fighting and damaging his property. But Station Shekhar assaulted Abdullah, who collapsed on the floor, bloodied with the deep gash on his head made by a machete. An onlooker called the police. By the time a sub-inspector and two constables reached the spot, Station Shekhar and his gang were getting into their cars, openly flashing their weapons. But the cops remained mute spectators like other locals. Savera was located close to the offices of the English daily *Deccan Herald* and the Kannada daily *Prajavani* on MG Road. By this time, news of the gang war reached the newsrooms and photographers of both the newspapers clicked pictures that proved to be extremely embarrassing for the Bengaluru Police. The pictures had captured the sub-inspector and the two constables standing in the crowd while the armed rowdies were fleeing in their cars. The police were shamed and there was anger building up among the citizens. Newspapers followed up the story with comments from enraged locals expressing concerns about their safety. Police Commissioner S.N.S. Murthy summoned the sub-inspector and the constables to question them about their roles. The apologetic policemen said that they had information that Station Shekhar was armed with a gun. The fear of being shot at prevented them from nabbing him, they reasoned. The cops suggested that a special squad be formed to nab him.

It had been three years since B.B. Ashok Kumar was shifted to law and order from the traffic police department following the success of 'Operation Tiger'. Ashok Kumar was roped in along with sub-inspectors Lava Kumar and N.D. Mulla to nab Station Shekhar. The special squad, including the seven constables, then started meticulously collecting information. Ashok Kumar, who was nicknamed Tiger, took it up as a challenge to trace Station Shekhar, just as he had done years ago when he had nabbed the chain snatchers.

'What is a case if it is not tough enough for us?' Ashok Kumar would say to himself.

Ashok Kumar belonged to the warrior community of Coorgis, who hail from the Kodagu district of Karnataka. They follow a peculiar tradition: every time a male child is born, he is welcomed with several rounds of firing. The baby is made to hold a bow and arrow to mark the beginning of his journey as a warrior. Every family in Kodagu district boasts of having at least seven to eight firearms and even the women are expert shooters. The tradition goes back to the time of Lord Mark Cubbon, who in the 1850s noticed the bravery of Coorg warriors and subsequently made an exception in the Disarmament Act for them. It meant that the natives of Coorg would never require a licence for acquiring a firearm.

Ashok Kumar and others in the squad met regularly to discuss the progress of the case. On 30 June 1989, exactly a month after Station Shekhar and his gang fled from Savera, one of the constables in the special squad traced the house of Kalapatthar, Station Shekhar's close accomplice. Kalapatthar had been untraceable since the murder at the railway station. The police had learnt of some activity in his house. They were hopeful of finding Station Shekhar there. But when they barged in, they only found Kalapatthar. He was dragged to the police station and interrogated in typical cop style. Soon he agreed to disclose the address of Station Shekhar's house. He accompanied the police squad, half of them plain-clothed, to Munegowda Road in Banaswadi, where Station Shekhar was holed up. The police made Kalapatthar knock on the door. A few seconds later, a window next to the door squeaked open slightly. Station Shekhar peeped out and spotted the policemen hiding on either side of the door. He switched off the lights inside the house. The police squad immediately became alert. Suddenly, the door flung open and two rounds were fired from inside the house. The police circled the house, their backs to the wall. A minute later, two more rounds were fired from inside while Station Shekhar ran from one end of the house to the other. Ashok Kumar, who had taken up position close to the door, spotted a figure moving around in the dark. In retaliation, he fired two rounds. For the next ten minutes, there was no action. The cops were scared that someone would fire again but there was absolutely no movement inside. After sometime, the policemen trooped in, each covering for the other. They switched on the lights only to find Station Shekhar lying in a pool of blood, lifeless. It was 2 a.m. on 1 July 1989. The Bengaluru Police had carried out its first encounter.

For a moment, the ten-member police squad was stunned. They had never been involved in killing a rowdy before. They tortured them during interrogations but had never killed one. And now, the squad was staring at a dead rowdy, bullets pierced into his body. They immediately informed a senior and a call was made to the commissioner informing him about the development. They carried out the basic spot duties and seized two countrymade revolvers with cartridges, a sword, a chopper and a knife from Station Shekhar's house.

'What case should we register?' Ashok Kumar asked the others in the squad, who stared at him blankly.

The forensic experts were summoned to the spot. In the meantime, the squad headed to Banaswadi Police Station, where they registered two cases against Station Shekhar—attempt to murder and obstructing a police officer on duty. The guidance came all the way from Mumbai. Senior police officers rang their counterparts who had already mastered encounters to stifle the growing terror of the underworld in Mumbai. The very first encounter in Mumbai had taken place way back in 1982, when police officer Isaque Bagwan and Raja Tambat had shot down gangster Manya Surve in Wadala, a central suburb of the city. The Mumbai Police officers were now seasoned players in encounters. The title 'encounter specialist' was already gaining as much popularity as the notoriety of the various criminal gangs in the country's financial capital. The cops took pride in killing the 'Bhais' as the rowdies were known as in Mumbai. But questions were being raised too. Many killings were termed as fake encounters. Allegations were made that cops were taking money from one criminal to eliminate another. Like Mumbai, Bengaluru too was destined to go down the same path but it was only the beginning.

As the day ended, the men in uniform were relieved that nothing had gone out of hand. The news of the encounter had made it to the front pages of all leading news dailies. Ashok Kumar, Lava Kumar and Mulla became heroes overnight with their interviews splashed in all newspapers. The excitement within the police force didn't die down for days after the incident. Other policemen often stopped members of the special squad and asked them to narrate the story, insisting that they not miss any detail. The *Times of India* wrote a story headlined 'Rowdy shot dead by police'. *Indian Express* reported: 'Wanted man opens fire, shot dead'. *Hindu* kept it straight. Its headline said, 'SI kills "rowdy"'. The entire city joined in praising the cops for killing Station Shekhar, who had become a menace after murdering Rajendra on the station premises. But at the end of the week, their triumph took a completely unexpected turn.

A complaint was filed at the Chief Metropolitan Magistrate's court by a woman named Vijaya alias Geetha against the ten policemen alleging that the encounter was actually a murder. Vijaya, a dancer at Hotel Revoli in Majestic, claimed that she was married to Station Shekhar and had a child with him. The police records maintained that Station Shekhar, who was thirty-two years old, had never married. Vijaya alleged that the cops barged into their Banaswadi home, handcuffed Station Shekhar and then shot him dead while she and her baby were in the house. She claimed to have been confined at the Banaswadi Police Station for a few days and later at the Kadugondanahalli Police Station. Vijaya's case was being fought by one of the most renowned lawyers in Bengaluru, Tomy Sebastian, who demanded that the case be transferred to the CBI for impartial investigation. What was not evident at this stage was that Vijaya was just a pawn whose controls were in the hands of Jayaraj. He had two interests in pursuing the case—Station Shekhar was his man and the accused were policemen, whom he considered his arch enemy.

During the investigation of the Rasheed murder case, the police had supported the arrested DCP and the others. They had also raised slogans against the CBI. Ashok Kumar was one of the cops at the helm of the protests. If the super sleuths from the CBI were to investigate the Station Shekhar encounter case, it was definitely not good news for Ashok Kumar and others. After the Rasheed murder case, the lawyers had decided against fighting any cases for the police. It was with much hard work that Ashok Kumar had finally managed to find a lawyer to fight for the accused DCP and the constables back then. Now, he needed a lawyer for himself and the other cops in his squad. But no one agreed.

Eventually the cops managed to convince well-known lawyer Santosh Hegde to appear for them. Santosh Hegde appealed in the higher court where the case was quashed and it was ordered that the matter be probed by a DCP.

As the inquiry began, a team of ballistics experts submitted a report that two rounds stuck in the door of Station Shekhar's house were fired from his Chinese made .33mm pistol. Further, the forensic team also submitted that gunshot residue, something which is produced after the combustion of the primer and the powder of the cartridge post-firing, was found on Station Shekhar's nails and skin. The ninety-day-long inquiry by the DCP concluded and a report was submitted to the commissioner. The report did not find any of the police officers guilty of murdering Shekhar. The news upset Jayaraj who was not expecting such an outcome. Through Vijaya and his lawyers, he appealed against the report and a fresh investigation by another DCP was ordered in the case.

The ten cops accused for the encounter of Station Shekhar were getting worried. They had not only risked their jobs but also their reputations. Every time Jayaraj made a move hiding behind his battery of lawyers and Vijaya, the cops would be on tenterhooks. They stood by each other, assuring themselves that nothing would go wrong. Whatever they had done was well within the bounds of their duty and that they would emerge clean. But some of them were furious at Jayaraj and thought he had crossed a line. After the Rasheed murder case, this was the second time Jayaraj had gone after the police. This time they were thinking of ways to bring Jayaraj down permanently.

14

Mumbai Mafia—Bengaluru's Nemesis

W eeks after Station Shekhar's encounter, a team of policemen stormed into Jayaraj's Wilson Garden residence armed with a search warrant. The police claimed to have received a tip-off about hidden arms and ammunition in Jayaraj's house. After an hour-long search, the police team came out jubilant. They had found a .303 rifle, a trigger and a barrel. They had also found twenty bottles of Scotch, a rare and expensive alcohol in those days, imported cigarettes, perfumes, a huge quantity of gold and silver ornaments and cash worth lakhs. The liquor bottles particularly brought smiles on their faces. Jayaraj, his younger brother Ramesh and two of his family members were immediately arrested. While the others were put in a police jeep and driven away as per protocol, the cops wanted to make a big show of Jayaraj's arrest. They wanted to make a statement that the underworld would never forget.

Jayaraj was chained and dragged out of his house in broad daylight. They pushed and hauled him till the police station. People had gathered in hordes to watch the show. The news had spread like wildfire. Some stopped their vehicles and some leaned out of their windows. To their utter shock, they found Jayaraj in chains. At a distance, Sreedhar, Bachchan and Varada too witnessed the march. It gave them goosebumps. Jayaraj was practically ruling Bengaluru at that time and had a force of over 2000 rowdies under him. His monthly earnings were rumoured to be between Rs 20 lakh and Rs 30 lakh. Needless to say, Jayaraj's arrest and the public humiliation had shaken Bengaluru.

'The police are not going to leave him,' Sreedhar told the other two in a voice overcome with emotion. 'They will go to any extent. This is perhaps his end.'

To weaken Jayaraj's hold on Bengaluru, he was shifted to Mysuru jail, while the other arrested members of his family were sent to Mangaluru jail. Interestingly, Jayaraj didn't protest against the police's brutish treatment even once. However, he instructed his gang members to start preparing for an election campaign. A few days later, he announced that he would be contesting in the upcoming by-elections from Jayanagar constituency. Jayaraj started conducting meetings from the prison. He meticulously planned the campaign and told his team members to give prominence to his Robin Hood image in order to win hearts and votes. He also began coaxing his contacts in the police force and in politics to allow him some time off from the jail for campaigning.

* * *

Back in Bengaluru, a dangerous plan was being hatched. It was decided that Jayaraj had to be eliminated. A unanimous decision was taken to entrust Rai with the job.

A few people approached him with a plan. All he had to do was execute the killing. But Rai demanded a valid reason for taking such a drastic step. The men knew well that killing a powerful don would only give birth to another, but they were still willing to risk it. It is said that some went out of their way to reason with Rai. When nothing seemed to convince him, Rai was told about DCP Narayan's arrest and how Jayaraj had become a menace for the police. Rai was even taken to the Coimbatore jail for further assurance. This time, Oil Kumar was introduced to Rai.

'I don't need any money, neither do I have any demands,' Rai told the men. 'I will kill Jayaraj.'

It was decided that Oil Kumar's money and manpower would back the entire operation. Rai believed that basic weapons like knives or machetes may not be enough to neutralize someone like Jayaraj. He decided to adopt the new ways that were popular in Mumbai.

'A gun would surely do the job,' he thought.

He got in touch with his Mumbai contacts to arrange for a firearm. It was planned that the execution would be carried out right outside the Mysuru jail when Jayaraj would return from a meeting of the All India Small and Medium Newspapers Federation in New Delhi, for which the court had granted him leave. The task of firing the gun was assigned to Bekinnakannu Rajendra. It was planned that Chakravarty alias Chakre, Agrahara Bachchan alias Bachchan, Mani Bharati, Krishnaki Rao alias Kitty, Renuka Acharya alias Kariya, Pushpa alias Lotus and Tamti Sanjeeva would then circle Jayaraj and attack him with swords, machetes and knives. A second gun was given to one of the boys in case things got out of control. A day before the attack, Rai took his gang of assassins to a secluded location to practise shooting as most of the men were handling a gun for the first time.

D-Day arrived. The group assembled early in the morning and took positions outside Mysuru jail. As the police vehicle carrying Jayaraj approached the jail premises, the men became alert. As soon as Jayaraj stepped out of the jeep, Bekinnakannu Rajendra fired a shot at him. But a novice in firing guns, he missed the target. Jayaraj swiftly ducked, missing the bullet by a few inches. He panicked and ran for cover behind the police jeep. But the attackers were too many. Within seconds, half a dozen men pounced on him. Jayaraj kicked and punched them even as a few deep gashes were made on him before he ran inside the jail premises. The second gun-bearing man did not even dare to pull out his weapon in front of Jayaraj. The failed plan left the men seething in anger.

Rai was burning with rage as he heard of the failed attack. The news travelled fast to Oil Kumar, who too lost his cool. The police were the most restless. Wasting no time on introspection, the group started planning another attack. This time it would be in the jail ward of Krishna Rajendra Hospital in Mysuru where Jayaraj was undergoing treatment for injuries sustained from the first attack. Jayaraj was on the second floor where two policemen guarded his room. Rai wanted to be doubly sure this time and leave nothing to chance. He contacted his acquaintances in Mumbai and arranged for four shooters. Additionally, Oil Kumar arranged for ten more men. Another four would come from Mangaluru through Rai's contacts. This time, they wanted the plan to be watertight.

The time of the attack was fixed at 6 a.m. As planned, the four shooters barged in and opened fire inside the hospital ward. But before any of the bullets could hit Jayaraj, he hurled several *kaccha* or crude bombs on them that he had sourced from his Naxalite links in Chittoor, Andhra Pradesh. He had hidden them under his bed. Jayaraj knew very well that another attack on his life was imminent and he was well-prepared. Though not fatal, the bombs did the trick of scaring the attackers who fled the spot. A thick cloud of black smoke had enveloped the hospital, spreading panic and chaos among the patients and the doctors; everyone ran for cover. Jayaraj had survived the second attack too, leaving Rai utterly humiliated.

* * *

Jayaraj chose a tiger as his election symbol. He often told his followers how he identified with the ferocious and powerful animal as they shared similar traits. In November 1989, Jayaraj's plea for a fifteen-day parole to campaign for the elections was accepted. His followers advised him to keep a low profile after the two near-fatal attempts on his life. But Jayaraj was adamant to go to any lengths to win the election.

His daily schedule would include making a stop at the Siddhapura Police Station to mark his attendance by signing a register before starting his tour of the area in an open jeep, hands folded graciously, sometimes waving at the people. He also brought a touch of quirk to his campaign. One morning, trailing his jeep was an open trolley with a shiny cage mounted on it. Inside the cage was a live tiger that he had borrowed from a circus for a hefty sum. As the news spread, people from every corner of the city flocked to see the big cat. The animal roared all along the way as Jayaraj smiled and waved at the spellbound crowd. To an outsider, it would seem as if Jayaraj had an enormous fan base. Hiring a tiger proved to be a masterstroke as it was not easy for an independent candidate to draw children and adults in such huge numbers.

Before Jayaraj was released on parole, Rai had been doing a recce of the stretch from Jayaraj's Wilson Garden residence to the Siddhapura Police Station every single day for two weeks. After two failed attempts, he had decided to take complete charge of the 'kill Jayaraj' operation. He would even jog in the area every morning to understand where Jayaraj could be accosted.

'The mission failed twice as the captain was in the back seat. This time, the captain will be at the forefront,' Rai announced.

Rai also sought the help of another contact from Mangaluru, Amar Alva. Alva, a charismatic, well-to-do man, enjoyed incredible power in Mangaluru and had connections with Mumbai's Shetty clan. He was the president of the All College Student's Union and enjoyed much clout due to this association. Alva also owned a permit room called Moti Mahal, a busy watering hole in Mangaluru. He owned a readymade garment store named Fashion Jungle in Hampankatta. At any given time, Alva moved around with more than twelve well-built men and a convoy of half a dozen cars. He had strong ties with Dawood Ibrahim's gang in Mumbai, mainly due to his contacts with two of Dawood Ibrahim's close aides—Ashok Shetty alias Ashok Lambu and Sharad Shetty—who smuggled gold from Dubai. Alva was their landing agent on the Mangaluru coast.

Alva put two of his hitmen from Mumbai, Subhash Singh Thakur and Francis Coutinho, on the job. A third shooter, Mangesh, was also roped in. The sharpest among the trio was Thakur, a dreaded sharpshooter from Dawood Ibrahim's gang. Thakur was inducted into the D-Gang by Sunil Sawant alias Sautya who was known as Dawood Ibrahim's *yamraj* (Lord of Death). They were trained in operating automatic weapons such as an AK-47, something that the Bengaluru rowdies had only heard of. Thakur could shoot a Kalashnikov using just one hand. A few years later, Thakur would go on to carry out the JJ Hospital shootout in Mumbai, where he would barge into a ward and gun down Shailesh Haldankar from the rival Arun Gawli gang to avenge the murder of Dawood Ibrahim's brother-in-law Ibrahim Ismail Parkar. Two policemen—P.G. Javsen and K.B. Bhanavat—would be killed in the firing while five others, including a nurse and a patient, would be severely injured.

Rai decided that the attack would take place when Jayaraj would be on his way to the Siddhapura Police Station. They would strike him at the Lalbagh back gate. Two motorcycles, an Ambassador and a Fiat were arranged to execute the killing. Rai decided that he would be on the spot this time to ensure that the task was accomplished. His close aide Jayant Rai also accompanied him.

On the morning of 21 November 1989, Jayaraj left for the routine police station visit in his Ambassador. His lawyer Vardhamanya sat next to him while his brother Umesh was at the wheel. As they reached the Lalbagh back gate, a Fiat blocked their way. Two motorcycles stopped on either side of Jayaraj's car, while an Ambassador stood at the rear. The attackers circled him and started shooting indiscriminately. Rai was in the lead. Vardhamanya was the first one to get hit. Jayaraj pulled the injured lawyer's body on to him and tried to use it as a shield to escape the bullets. He also hurled a few bombs that he always kept handy. But his end was inevitable this time. He was grievously injured as several bullets pierced through his body. He stopped breathing. An eerie silence fell over the place as the dance of death finally ended. The attackers swiftly got into their vehicles and fled. Jayaraj's brother Umesh was the only one to survive. For the first time, Bengaluru had woken up to the sound of gunshots that had permanently silenced Jayaraj.

* * *

The news sent shockwaves through the Bengaluru crime world. After the necessary procedures, Jayaraj's body was brought to his Wilson Garden residence and kept for public viewing. As many as 10,000 people gathered on the first day. The last rites were delayed by four days as his brother Ramesh, who was in jail, was not permitted leave immediately. Most of Jayaraj's gang members went underground assuming that the police would hunt them down like dogs now that their leader was dead. Curiosity had gripped the underworld. Everyone wanted to know who had killed Jayaraj. Rai's name had begun to do the rounds, but nobody could confirm his involvement. Meanwhile, as a part of the larger conspiracy between the killers of Jayaraj, Bekinnakannu Rajendra and Pushpa—who were a part of the squad that had made the first failed attempt to kill Jayaraj outside Mysuru jail—were picked up to show that a speedy investigation was going on. What the common man didn't know was that the so-called killer duo was not even present in Bengaluru on the day of the attack as they were lodged in the Chikmagalur jail for creating nuisance in a bar. Bekinnakannu Rajendra and Pushpa could use that ground to steer clear of the murder charges later in the court.

Rai went underground. The shooters from Mumbai had also dispersed to different locations. Oil Kumar called for grand celebrations. They cheered, laughed and gloated in their victory, calling it an end of the Maharaja's rule. It was also curtains down for *Garibi Hatavo*.

15

Mumbai Bhais in Bhugataloka

The deafening gunshots that reverberated across Karnataka were accompanied by an insistent question: Who was Muthappa Rai?

Rai had single-handedly paved the way for the Mumbai mafia to enter Bengaluru. Getting help from Mumbai's sharpshooters also meant that thereafter, the Kannadiga rowdies could seek assistance from the financial capital that boasted of Dawood Ibrahim, the king of the underworld, and some of the deadliest gangsters who worked under him. More importantly, the Bengaluru mafia had reasons to believe that Rai had close ties with Dawood Ibrahim.

In reality, it was Dawood Ibrahim's close aide Sharad Shetty, who was friends with Rai. Sharad Anna, as he was known in the underworld, was a small-time jeweller from Jogeshwari, a suburb in Mumbai. While most Shettys who hailed from Dakshin

Kannada district of Karnataka entered the restaurant business that was big on money, Sharad Anna ran a jewellery shop. He made enough money but not as much as he would have liked. Sharad Anna was not so much bothered about the means as he was about the end. He took to smuggling gold into the city and over time came in contact with Dawood Ibrahim in 1979. Dawood Ibrahim and Sharad Anna began smuggling gold by air. The modus operandi was simple. They would hire people to bring in gold from Dubai and dump it in a dustbin at Mumbai airport before reaching the customs frisking booths. The gold, mostly in the form of biscuits, would be packed in sweet boxes. Soon a sweeper, on their pay roll, would clear the bins and hand over the gold to them outside the airport. This strategy was code-named garbage line, sweeper line or the *kachra-peti* line. It was the most lucrative business till Indian customs officials busted it in 1981. The investigators seized gold biscuits worth over Rs 25 lakh and interrogations led them to Dawood Ibrahim, Sharad Anna, and other men who worked for the duo. They were charged under COFEPOSA (Conservation of Foreign Exchange and Prevention of Smuggling Activities Act, 1974) and lodged at Arthur Road Jail. They pulled strings to get out of prison and in no time, they were back to smuggling. Simultaneously, they had expanded to drug trafficking.

In 1984, when Dawood Ibrahim escaped to Dubai, Sharad Anna went in tow. He entered into flesh trade, bought five hotels in Dubai, ventured into cricket betting and quickly rose to become the drug trafficking kingpin in Dubai.

With Rai's increasing clout in Bengaluru, Sharad Anna was hopeful that he could now spread his wings in Bengaluru and Mangaluru. Dawood Ibrahim too wanted to expand his empire to another city. For him, there were hardly any new avenues in Mumbai.

It was Rai's connection that made the Mumbai bhais feel at home in Karnataka. All of a sudden, the Bengaluru and Mangaluru police began to get complaints about extortion and other petty criminal activities involving the Mumbai annas. But the clever dons would always find a way to camouflage their actions by giving the police the impression that they were simply visiting their hometowns and were not involved in any mischief. In reality, extorting money or brokering deals were only means of exploring ways to spread their networks in their hometowns and gauge the law and order situation. The cops began hearing of cases of several underhand real estate deals and extortion threats, something that the Mumbai mafia was known for but never the rowdies of Bengaluru. These were early signs of the Mumbai underworld gaining an entry into Karnataka. The police activated their information networks to gather intelligence on the Mumbai underworld. The coastal areas of Mangaluru and Karwar were also put under close surveillance.

Rai, who had gained mega stardom in the underworld after Jayaraj's murder, did not hesitate in offering a helping hand to the Mumbai dons. They could rely on him when they were down south. In the meantime, two more murders put Rai on the list of the most wanted gangsters in Karnataka. Incidentally, his next victim would be as influential as his first one.

Sharad Anna's plans to expand to Bengaluru were not hidden from Rai. It was Rai who had introduced Oil Kumar to Sharad Anna during the planning of Jayaraj's murder. However, Oil Kumar later started directly contacting Sharad Anna. This did not go down well with Rai.

After Jayaraj's murder, one after another, all the rowdies from the city began aligning with Rai. Sreedhar and Bachchan too joined hands with him. Jointly, they decided to get rid of Oil Kumar. But Oil Kumar was not an easy target. Rai, who had now become 'MR' for the underworld, would call him Brutus Kumar. A complex character in William Shakespeare's *Julius Caesar*, Brutus was someone Caesar trusted, but who ended up leading the group that killed Caesar. Sreedhar, who addressed Rai as Muthappa Anna, was immediately convinced that Oil Kumar needed to be eliminated as he was capable of scheming and killing them all. Oil Kumar's elimination would mean that the powers of Bengaluru would come wholly to Rai, who already had Jayaraj's murder under his belt. Sreedhar, now his close aide, was also on a high, post Kotwal's murder. They all agreed that in order to kill Oil Kumar, a unique strategy had to be devised. They started keeping a close watch on Oil Kumar while ensuring that they remained in his good books. Oil Kumar's penchant for alcohol and women would be taken care of by

Rai and Sreedhar. The duo pampered Oil Kumar in all their parties thinking it was the best way to gain his trust.

They rented a large house with a garden in HSR Layout. Their plan was to bury Oil Kumar alive. They dug a pit in the garden and installed mosaic tiles inside. They intended to push Oil Kumar into the pit after inviting him over on the pretext of a party. The slippery tiles would prevent him from climbing out of the pit. After all the arrangements were made, they invited Oil Kumar over. But the suspicious Oil Kumar did not turn up.

The failure of the plan, however, didn't dissuade the duo. They began thinking of other ways when an idea struck Rai. He got Sharad Anna to call Oil Kumar for a meeting in Sadashivanagar.

Oil Kumar took great pride in having direct contact with Sharad Anna as he felt closer to the D-Gang. When Sharad Anna called him from Dubai to say that he was in Bengaluru and wanted to meet him, Oil Kumar was least suspicious. But he had lied as he had never left Dubai. On 20 November 1990, Oil Kumar went alone to a residential building in Sadashivanagar to meet Sharad Anna. Bachchan and two other men, armed with machetes and choppers, had taken position. As soon as Oil Kumar stepped out of his car, the three men attacked him and pinned him down. After a few stabs, Oil Kumar stopped breathing.

No one knew what Oil Kumar looked like. He was identified several hours after his murder by a police officer. When a case of murder was registered, a watchman from a nearby plot in his statement said that he had heard a man shouting, 'Umesha, no Umesha'. Umesh was the name of Jayaraj's younger brother. This was, of course, a ploy to make Oil Kumar's murder look like a revenge killing. But the investigations revealed that Umesh was in a police station at the time of the murder after he was caught for a traffic violation while riding his motorcycle. When the police took down the statement of Oil Kumar's wife Rita, she fearlessly told them, 'Rai was my husband's enemy.' This shifted the police's focus to Rai.

After Jayaraj's murder, a notorious rowdy named H.M. Krishna Murthy alias Jederahalli Krishnappa tried to project himself as the next don. He became notorious after killing another rowdy named Semene Siddha. But after eliminating Oil Kumar, Rai had not left any scope for anyone. He was now the undisputed leader of Bengaluru's crime world and enjoyed unparalleled clout. The others had to be content with playing second fiddle.

A year after Oil Kumar's killing, Rai's named cropped up in an FIR of another high-profile murder—the killing of Amar Alva.

Rai had sought Alva's help in Jayaraj's killing. But the Mumbai and Bengaluru boys who were involved in the operation were yet to see the money. When they approached Rai for their share, he told them to go to Alva, stating that since the contract was given to him, the money too was handed over to him. When the boys approached Alva, he appeared to be shocked. He said that he had not received a single penny from Rai. This created a huge rift between the two dons. The Mumbai boys trusted Alva given that Francis Coutinho, who was one of the shooters, was a close friend of his. The Bengaluru boys did not trust Rai, neither did Alva. Between the negotiations, the news of Alva's murder suddenly made the headlines and the first suspect was Rai.

Alva, who was the landing agent for Ashok Shetty and Sharad Anna, was facing music from Ashok Shetty over a huge consignment of gold worth Rs 6 crore that was to land on the coast near Hoige Bazaar in Mangaluru. They were unaware that the customs officials and the Pandeshwar police had been tipped-off about the landing. Plain-clothed sleuths from both the departments kept a close watch on the coast, completely unaware that they were working on the same tip-off. When both sides found out, it led to a heated argument between the two departments. Alva, who got wind of the bickering among the officials, shifted the landing location to Calicut in Kerala. Alva and twenty-six of his men left for Calicut to land the gold but the customs officials and the cops managed to stay a step ahead of them. They had already taken positions and as soon as the boats were harboured, the police overpowered the gangsters and seized the booty. Ashok Shetty was left fuming over the huge loss and demanded that Alva reimburse him. In response, Alva said that it was part and parcel of their business and that he could not be held responsible. This incident led to a crack in their relationship. Ashok Shetty now wanted Alva dead.

A hawala dealer, Prabhakar Shetty, who was active in Mumbai and Mangaluru, was robbed of Rs 6 lakh by Yathish Shetty, a crook from Kapu village in Udupi district. An angry Prabhakar Shetty gave Alva a contract to kill Yathish Shetty. Alva and his gang members barged into Yathish Shetty's house and demanded the money at knifepoint. But Yathish Shetty managed to escape and fled to Mumbai, where he met Ashok Shetty through local contacts, and offered to eliminate Alva. Ashok Shetty gave him a huge sum of money, a car, and two revolvers to Yathish Shetty. A few weeks later, Yathish Shetty headed back to Kankanadi in Mangaluru, where he started keeping a close watch on Alva's movements. One day, he learnt that Alva was hosting a grand celebration for his daughter's first birthday and that he would come to a bakery near Milagres Church to collect the cake a day earlier. Yathish Shetty and two of his accomplices, Shrikara and Murali, parked their car near the bakery and waited patiently for their target to arrive. On 18 December 1991, around 6.45 p.m., Alva arrived with his entourage. Yathish Shetty and Shrikara, who were armed with revolvers, started firing indiscriminately as soon as Alva stepped out of the car, while Murali attacked with his sword. This was the first time Mangaluru had heard gunshots in its galis. One bullet hit Alva who ran for his life. Yathish Shetty ran after him followed by Shrikara, who was still firing, Murali in tow. By then, Alva was hit with two more bullets and he collapsed near Rajkamal Hotel. But one of Shrikara's bullets hit Yathish Shetty as well. In a state of panic, they put Yathish Shetty in an autorickshaw and rushed him to nearby Kilpady village where Ashok Shetty's brother Balesh Shetty lived. From there, Yathish Shetty was taken to a local hospital while the duo was left in a thick forested area between Karkala and Moodabidri. Balesh Shetty arranged for food and some bed sheets and asked them to stay put. Every night, a jeep from Surathkal would bring them food and other supplies in the jungle.

Back in Mangaluru, the Mulki police registered the case of Alva's murder and named Rai as the first suspect. Rai was interrogated by police officer Lava Kumar at the Puttur inspection bungalow to track his involvement. Lava Kumar had known Rai since the latter's days as a clerk in Vijaya Bank in Puttur. When he started questioning, Rai defiantly denied his role. Lava Kumar pulled out Rai's call records by visiting Videsh Sanchar Nigam Limited at Madras and Mumbai but they too did not point towards his involvement. While his interrogation continued, the Mulki police received a tip-off about a jeep leaving from Surathkal every night. They apprehended the driver, who spilled the beans. Six days after Alva's murder, the police caught Shrikara and Murali. Yathish Shetty was arrested from the hospital. Eventually, Rai's name was cleared in the case. But Alva's relatives and gang members believed that Rai had told the police to clear his name. One day, a close relative of Alva met Lava Kumar and asked him a question.

'Where is your brain?' Lava Kumar was shocked at this arrogant question.

'What do you mean?' he asked angrily.

The relative replied, 'Do you know where Muthappa Rai's brain is? It starts from his head and goes down to his toes. It is not easy to catch him.'

The police had given Rai a clean chit, but Alva's friends wanted revenge.

16

Neophytes Battle for Supremacy

Rai vehemently defended himself in crime circles that he had nothing to do with Alva's murder, but he was well aware that sooner or later the heat of the investigation would turn against him. He thought of using his police contacts to get into jail by manipulating records, which would show that he was behind bars at the time of the killing. But it did not work out as Rai was well known and couldn't have landed in prison unnoticed. None of the policemen agreed to take the risk despite being offered large sums of money. He then rang up Sreedhar and asked him to make some arrangement. Sreedhar picked up Rai on his motorcycle and drove him to Jayadeva Institute of Cardiology where he was admitted with 'chest pain'.

Alva's murder, however, had sowed a doubt in Sreedhar's mind just as in everybody else's. He was not sure if Rai was trustworthy. While Sreedhar bragged about

Rai being a close friend, the latter rarely reciprocated the enthusiasm, always reiterating that Sreedhar was only playing second fiddle to him.

Setting aside their trust issues, the duo worked together for a year and a half making hefty amounts from the oil business, through extortion and protection money. They had also started raking in huge profits by brokering real estate deals and settling land disputes outside courts. But soon enough, differences started to crop up in their partnership.

Rai was ambitious and authoritarian. He wanted to be the sole power centre in Bengaluru and a one-point contact. Bengaluru had several smaller groups of rowdies who had earlier owed allegiance to Kotwal, Jayaraj or Oil Kumar. All these groups were now under Rai, and Sreedhar played the middleman as he had more ground-level contacts.

Rai ensured that none of the groups mingled with each other and they directly coordinated with him. Sreedhar believed that Rai was following what his mentors from Mumbai and Dubai had taught him: never let smaller groups interact with each other. Sreedhar, on the other hand, thought that having one large group was the best approach as everyone could be under the same umbrella. He believed that small, fragmented groups could lead to misunderstandings and internal fights. Rai was completely opposed to the idea and conveyed it to Sreedhar in as many words. Another thing that bothered Sreedhar was Rai's bias towards men from Mumbai and the Bunt community.

Rai worked out of a small office on Brigade Road. Sreedhar and Bachchan were among the daily visitors. On days when he had time to spare, he would take all the boys to a farmhouse in Madikeri and organize cockfights for them. He loved the intensity of this sport and the competitive spirit it brought out in the boys.

Around the same time, M. Kempaiah, an exceptionally tough cop, was posted as Bengaluru's DCP in the southern region of the city. Already popular in Bijapur and Shivamogga for his drive against rowdies, Kempaiah's appointment made Rai sweat. He came to know that Kempaiah was actively collecting information on him.

Such was Rai's fear of Kempaiah that on days when he got to know that the DCP was in the area, he would pull down the shutters of his office. It is said that rowdies and top dons tried everything to bribe Kempaiah but he would term the offers as 'dust on his shoes'. On one occasion, when Rai went to meet Kempaiah on Sreedhar's insistence, the strict cop curtly ordered him to button up his shirt. Fear of Kempaiah drove Rai to build his contacts with politicians. Rai harboured a constant fear that Kempaiah would kill him in an encounter.

Sreedhar and the smaller gangs had started meeting up regularly to discuss how they could operate in Bengaluru without Rai's interference. The popular suggestion was that they should all join hands and get rid of Rai. Sreedhar, however, did not want to be tagged as the 'betrayer' twice over. He had killed Kotwal after winning his trust. He did not want a repeat of that with Rai. He suggested that he would meet Kempaiah and tell him that the gangs had decided to part ways with Rai. That way in case a major crime was committed by Rai or his boys, the other gangs would remain safe. The gangs then decided to announce their break up with Rai officially and follow Sreedhar's plan. Several smaller groups came together and went to each and every club in the city to announce that the Bengaluru gangs had united and all the mamool should come to them. Rai was now one against many. Meanwhile, he received information about Sreedhar's meeting with Kempaiah and suspected that something was brewing against him. Even as the heat around Alva's murder died down, Rai stayed away from Bengaluru, making only secret visits when needed.

One afternoon, Sreedhar received a call from Rai.

'Hello Sreedhar, the former don is calling Bengaluru's current don. Feels good, doesn't it? Congratulations,' he said.

Sreedhar went blank for a moment. He gathered his thoughts and answered casually.

'How are you?'

'Why, Sreedhar? Why did you have to insult me by making a show at all the clubs? You are bragging about chasing me away from Bengaluru,' Rai raised his voice.

'All the gangs decided to unite. It was a joint decision. How long was I supposed to fight in your shadow?' Sreedhar retorted.

Rai laughed. 'You are overconfident because you have Kempaiah's support. You can keep your Bengaluru.

But ensure that my boys are not troubled,' he said before disconnecting the call.

Fearing an attack by Rai, Sreedhar shifted from his Girinagar house to a rented place in ISRO Layout. To avoid suspicion, he put up a board outside the house that read 'SM Associates, Land Developers'. With Rai away from Bengaluru, Sreedhar and his gang were flooded with deals. Money was flowing in from all quarters. It was said that the gangs would rake in more than Rs 15 lakh a month. But, they never completely forgot Rai and kept trying to gather information about his activities and hideouts. One could never get too overconfident after all. Suddenly one morning, the newspapers reported that Rai had been arrested from Heggadadevana kote in Mysuru district. The police seized a pistol from him and lodged him in Mysuru jail. He was brought for the hearings to Bengaluru in a police van with tight security. Rumours were that Rai wore a bulletproof vest every time he stepped out in the open.

On 12 April 1993, Rai was brought to the city sessions court in the morning. Suddenly, a man dressed like an advocate walked up close to him and pulled out a pistol from under his coat. Rai was shot at close range. He collapsed in a pool of blood. Barely conscious, he slid below the police van to save himself. He also called out to the public to help him and take him to a hospital. The attacker, Narayan Salian, began to run but was overpowered by a few onlookers and a police constable near the gate. Four others who had accompanied Salian managed to escape.

Five bullets had pierced through Rai's arm, hips and chest. He was rushed to the nearby St Martha's Hospital and later shifted to Victoria Hospital after his condition stabilized. In the hospital, when Rai regained consciousness briefly, he insisted that the cops take down his statement at once. He said that DCP Kempaiah was behind the attack. He also said that he could be targeted again in the hospital and thus needed security. Rai's advocate, C.H. Hanumantharaya, echoed his thoughts.

'The attack on my client was due to lack of security provided by the police to him. A particular police officer was hell-bent on producing him in court though we did not want his physical presence here. We could have dispensed the case even without Muthappa Rai being actually present here,' Hanumantharaya told the *Times of India*. The article was headlined 'Advocate shoots gangster'.

Rai's wife Reca gave a letter to Chief Minister Veerappa Moily stating that some senior police officers were after her husband's life and claimed that they were working hand in glove with Rai's rivals. His advocate alleged that earlier when his client was brought to the court, elaborate security arrangements were made. But on the day of the attack, there was a blatant lapse.

'Usually when Rai was brought in the police van, the vehicle would halt near the staircase close to the advocates' recreation room. The same was expected this time and many of Rai's gang members waited for him there. But out of the blue, they decided to take the vehicle straight to the other staircase where the crowd was thin. That was where Salian was waiting, dressed in a lawyer's robe,' Hanumantharaya told the press, demanding that the investigations be handed over to either the Corps of Detectives or to the CBI as the local police would never be able to hunt down the real culprits.

The Ulsoorgate police had started interrogating Salian. It turned out that he was a barber from Mangaluru. He confessed that the attack was a revenge killing of Alva's murder and was masterminded by Alva's close friend Francis Coutinho. He and his gang also held a grudge against Rai for not paying them for Jayaraj's murder. After Jayaraj's murder, Mangesh, one of the sharpshooters, was arrested in Mumbai in another case. The gang had then approached Oil Kumar for Rs 5 lakh to release Mangesh. But Oil Kumar too had told them that all the money was given to Rai. Salian was to shoot Rai in the head but it turned out that he was in a heavily inebriated state and couldn't aim properly.

All the gangs of Bengaluru kept their fingers crossed hoping that Rai would succumb to the injuries. But he survived.

* * *

In Bengaluru's Muslim underworld, newbies attempted to establish their supremacy over Koli Faiyaz's rule. Koli Faiyaz was in jail while his trusted man Tanveer was busy hoodwinking the cops leaving Shivajinagar in the hands of budding criminals.

One of them was Rizwan Baig alias Rizwan Moula. Rizwan Moula's right hand was Chappal Hameed, who was dying to avenge his brother Yunus's murder that was ordered by Koli Faiyaz from jail. Koli Faiyaz claimed that he had only ordered a half-murder, but Yunus turned out to be too weak and succumbed to his injuries. Rizwan Moula and Chappal Hameed gradually took over Koli Faiyaz's business and ensured that all the mamool came to them. Koli Faiyaz could do little from behind bars.

In the beginning of 1995, Koli Faiyaz walked out of jail and began recouping with his gang. He managed to gain control of his businesses and sent out his gang members to announce that he was back and would not spare anyone if the mamool went anywhere else.

He had a fixed routine. Before going to his poultry shop, he would walk past Shivajinagar Police Station on Broadway Road and stop at a tiny paan shop to buy cigarettes. He would light one and then walk the rest of the way smoking the cigarette. Rizwan Moula, Chappal Hameed and their gang members Babu Pandey and Aslam Bali had been closely watching Koli Faiyaz's movements. On the morning of 8 June 1995, after Koli Faiyaz lit his cigarette, Aslam Bali approached him with a friendly smile.

'Salaam,' he said and threw chilli powder into Koli Faiyaz's eyes.

Before Koli Faiyaz could recover from the stinging sensation, Rizwan Moula and the others attacked him with a chopper and a sword. Koli Faiyaz collapsed in a pool of blood while the attackers disappeared. No eyewitnesses dared to open their mouths. Most of them were shopkeepers whom Koli Faiyaz had harassed for years. They were happy to be back in business, with no monopoly.

Koli Faiyaz's death shocked his followers. An erstwhile member of his gang, in an interview with me, said that a local MLA who was supported by Koli Faiyaz could not stop crying when he saw his lifeless body at the Victoria Hospital morgue. But his murder led to the rise of his close aide Tanveer, who vowed to take revenge.

Exactly six months after Koli Faiyaz's death, Tanveer and fourteen of his men kidnapped one Mohammad Farooq from Bharathinagara and killed him with sickles and knives. Farooq was a close follower of Rizwan Moula and Chappal Hameed, and was the brain behind Koli Faiyaz's murder. By killing Farooq, Tanveer wanted to send a strong signal that he was the new boss of Shivajinagar.

Tanveer then fled to Mumbai. He got married to a woman named Fahmida from Mumbra, a distant suburb predominantly populated by Muslims. Eight months later when Tanveer returned to Bengaluru to prepare for a dacoity, the City Crime Branch (CCB) team nabbed him and sent him to judicial custody in Gulbarga jail, about 600 kilometres from Bengaluru.

By this time, Tanveer had over forty cases lodged against him. From robbing as little as Rs 150 to extorting huge amounts from bar owners, assaulting with mini razors to killing with sickles, Tanveer's name had appeared in a number of crimes across the city. Tanveer's clout could be gauged by the fact that he managed to get himself transferred from Gulbarga jail to Mysuru jail and later to Bengaluru Central Jail so that he could conduct his business by staying in close proximity, and also plan his escape.

One day after complaining of a severe headache, Tanveer was taken to NIMHANS for check-up in a police van at around 11.45 a.m. When Tanveer got out of the van, six men held the police at gunpoint and dragged Tanveer into a white Maruti and sped away.

But according to a police report made later, the story was completely different. It was stated that from NIMHANS, Tanveer told the cops that he wanted to meet his mother and promised to return early. The police escort believed him and accompanied him. Tanveer entered a house belonging to one K.T. Babu near Wilson Garden and escaped through the rear door. He was eventually caught after a forty-five-day-long manhunt.

The incident laid bare the nexus between the criminals, the police and the jail staff. An inquiry report to track the lapses in the jails mentioned how Tanveer had close associations with select escort personnel with whom he remained friendly, providing them with food and pocket money.

'Tanveer and his accomplices had won over some escort policemen. They had a personal rapport with these men. Whenever he was being taken from Bengaluru Central Jail to the court or to the hospitals, these policemen would accompany him. On the way, he would stop at resorts to hold meetings, settle deals and conduct his businesses,' the report stated.

Such was his hold over the police and other authorities that he had got a steel grille made around his cell for his personal safety at his own expense. In the cell, he operated safely, making lakhs of rupees by meeting his fellow gang members, taking business decisions and even solving land disputes.

During his stay in all the three jails, Tanveer enjoyed having food of his choice delivered from expensive restaurants or from his home. It is said that the extortion money was brought to him in the jail, which he used to bribe the policemen and jail authorities.

For the gangsters, the police escorts came cheap. It is said that Tanveer paid Rs 150 to Rs 200 to get his desired police escort, and Rs 200 to the jail guard to let him move freely, talk and hold meetings.

To gain popularity among the inmates, Tanveer had once ordered food worth Rs 19,000 during Dussehra. During the month of Ramzan, he spent Rs 40,000 to provide fruits and food for fasting Muslim inmates. He attempted to portray the image of a do-gooder, a trait his idol Amitabh Bachchan had in many of his films.

* * *

A few months after being discharged from hospital, Rai got bail. He lived in a farmhouse at Madikeri. Only the most trusted members of his gang knew about the location. Money had dried up as Sreedhar and other gangs had taken over. Rai slowly started recovering his lost ground but his aggression was missing. Not much later, his name cropped up as the prime suspect in the murder of a rowdy named Balaram, who was lodged in Bengaluru jail, and for the killing of a timber merchant in Madikeri. But before the police could zero in on Rai, he fled to Dubai.

17

Bhugataloka's Bedlam in Bangkok

In Dubai, Rai finally felt safe. He was now under Sharad Anna's protection and no one could touch him. Sharad Anna's Jumeirah Beach residence was Rai's regular hangout. Although life was peaceful, he was unhappy to have left Bengaluru in the hands of Sreedhar and gang. He would often think of ways to reclaim his position back home. Eliminating the competition seemed to be the only way to achieve what he desired.

In July 1997, barely a year after Rai had escaped to Dubai, he planned to attack Sreedhar. He got his close aide Bannanje Raje to keep an eye on Sreedhar's movements. He found out that Sreedhar lived in Kumaraswamy Layout. The shooters lingered around his residence for days together searching for the right opportunity to strike. Suddenly one morning, they spotted a car leaving the compound. The driver was a balding man of average build. Without much thought, Bannanje Raje and two of his accomplices fired indiscriminately and fled the scene, ignorant of the fact that they had actually gunned down Sreedhar's driver Seena, who looked strikingly similar to his boss. Bachchan and another man, who were in the car, escaped with injuries. Although Sreedhar was alive, Rai was happy to find his name doing the rounds in the crime world once again.

Sreedhar's gang members were infuriated. They coaxed their leader to retaliate but he was too preoccupied with an image makeover. He now wanted to lead a reformed life. His right-hand man Bachchan too had decided to follow in his footsteps. To his punters, Sreedhar's transformation seemed ludicrous as instead of planning a retribution, he was brainstorming to find a suitable name for a weekly newspaper that he was planning to launch. After much brainstorming, he decided to call it 'Agni' (fire). From Sreedhar Murthy, he came to be known as Agni Sreedhar.

Rai had a hearty laugh when he learnt of Sreedhar's new venture. He saw it as an opportunity to expand his empire in Dubai while maintaining his grip on Bengaluru. Rai ventured into the hospitality sector and started Alf Castle, a plush hotel in Dubai, and went on to expand his trade in Kazakhstan by starting a family restaurant. He simultaneously dabbled in the electronic business. He also travelled to South Africa, Saudi Arabia and Russia to explore opportunities in the pharmaceutical business. With money flowing in from multiple quarters, Rai bought a plush villa in Bur Dubai and shifted there with his family.

To settle matters back home, he thought it was important to be more accessible and created an email ID, *nimagaggi@hotmail.com*, that was passed on to people in Bengaluru and Mangaluru. In Kannada, nimagaggi means 'for you'. His gang circulated the email ID, urging those who needed assistance in settling disputes or misunderstandings to write to Muthappa Anna. Rai called it his social venture and boasted of receiving 400 emails every day. He bragged about solving 60 per cent of the issues by simply making calls from Dubai. The rest were left to his Bengaluru boys.

Rai's eyes were very much on Bengaluru where Sreedhar, though away from the underworld, had started meddling in several real estate deals and making a lot of money.

On 21 December 1999, a sharpshooter from Mumbai, Eric Daniel, was shot in a police encounter. It was said that Daniel, a supari killer, was sent by Rai to establish himself in Bengaluru and eliminate Sreedhar at some point.

No matter what Rai did, he couldn't get closer to Dawood Ibrahim. But opportunities have a strange way of presenting themselves.

Chhota Rajan, a Hindu don, had parted ways with Dawood Ibrahim soon after the 1993 serial blasts in Mumbai. Both the dons were baying for each other's blood. More than one hundred gang members from each side had died in this gang war as their enmity continued to deepen. Anyone who wanted to be in their good books would pass on information of their rivals.

Once, Mumbai gangsters Ravi Poojary and Guru Satam were overheard talking about Chhota Rajan in a Dubai restaurant. Heavily intoxicated, the two were heard boasting about their ability to get information on Rajan's hideout if someone gave them good money. The duo, who had started out as extortionists, had earlier worked for Chhota Rajan before forming their own gang. They were hiding in Dubai after the Mumbai Police had launched a manhunt for them in several cases, including murders. Their conversation was overheard by a man in the restaurant who knew Rai. He immediately rang him up and told him about Poojary and Satam's drunken banter. Within an hour, Rai arrived at the restaurant and sat down in front of the two men.

After exchanging pleasantries, he came straight to the point.

'What do you know about Chhota Rajan?' he asked. The two men smiled slyly.

'Do you know where he is hiding?' Rai asked.

The duo kept smiling. 'Paanch crore (Rs 5 crore),' Poojary said flashing his palm in front of Rai's face.

Rai thought that this could be a jackpot. He did not bargain at all. Instead, as a token for the deal, he took Poojary and Satam to a nearby mall and shopped for them, the bill exceeding 40,000 dirhams. From there, Rai headed straight to Sharad Anna's Jumeirah Beach house and shared the information with excitement. Sharad Anna rang Dawood Ibrahim's Karachi-based lieutenant, Chhota Shakeel, who in turn informed the big daddy. He agreed to pay the amount but said that Rs 1 crore would be paid as advance while the remaining money would be given only after the information was verified. Not wanting to take a chance, he sent his own men to carry out the hit.

After they reached an agreement, Poojary and Satam parted with the most valuable information: the address of Chhota Rajan's hideout.

Sawan Court,
Soi 26, Sukhumvit,
Bangkok, Thailand

Dawood Ibrahim formed a team of seven lieutenants and at the helm was Rashid Hussain Sheikh alias Rashid Malbari. Malbari had a personal score to settle with Chhota Rajan, whose men had killed his brother Sajid in 1997 in the most savage manner. Sajid was beheaded in broad daylight. In a police statement, Malbari had described his brother's brutal killing as the turning point in his life. Dawood Ibrahim sent his team to Bangkok and arranged for seven weapons and 800 rounds. The group rented a house in Aree Court, a building opposite Sawan Court. They kept a close watch on Rajan's movements. He hardly ever stepped out of his apartment, they realized. After patiently gathering intelligence for weeks, they planned the first attack outside a five-star hotel where Chhota Rajan was headed for a meeting and to spend some leisure time. Dawood Ibrahim's gang fanned out near the hotel, securing every entry and exit. But when Rajan arrived, none of them could muster the courage to pull the trigger. The first attempt was an embarrassing failure.

They planned the second attack in his house. Sawan Court was a gated community comprising three buildings, each of five storeys. The flat was rented by Chhota Rajan's trusted soldier Rohit Verma, who lived there with his wife. A small-time robber from Mumbai's Vakola area, Verma had graduated to become Chhota Rajan's foremost sharpshooter. While his family owned a stationery shop, Verma lacked the patience for slow earnings. He formed a small gang and started committing robberies. He soon caught Chhota Rajan's eye and was trained in handling guns only to become his top shooter in the years to come.

The residents of Sawan Court were oblivious to the presence of a gangster amidst them. Dawood Ibrahim ordered his men to be better prepared for the second attack. He ordered them to make the assault a success at any cost. A date was fixed, 14 September 2000. Malbari and his men, dressed in crisp black suits, walked into the building, carrying a box of cake. They also had two Thai men accompanying them. Dawood Ibrahim had laid down yet another condition.

'Put the gun on his forehead and call me. I want him to know that I could kill him anytime,' Dawood Ibrahim ordered his men.

They rang the doorbell. Verma opened the door and froze. Before he could react, Malbari and his gang gunned him down. His wife, who came running out, was shot at once and left injured. But Chhota Rajan was nowhere to be seen. The men figured out that he had locked himself inside the bedroom. They began firing at the door. As many as eighty rounds were fired, of which one hit Chhota Rajan in the abdomen. Chhota Rajan knew that if he stayed inside the house, he would die. So he decided to make a run for his life. He jumped off the bedroom's low-rise balcony and landed on his feet, fracturing his ankle. With the sound of gunfire booming in the building, Malbari feared that the Thai police might soon arrive at the scene. He and his men fled the spot without waiting to check if Chhota Rajan was inside the bedroom or whether the bullets had hit him. They desperately hoped that the spray of bullets had killed him. The unsuspecting residents of the building ran to help Chhota Rajan and rushed him to Samitivej Hospital in a *tuk tuk* (rickshaw). It was only a day later that the residents learnt that what they had witnessed was a full-blown gang war between two of Mumbai's most-dreaded gangsters.

Dawood Ibrahim was furious. Malbari asked for his permission to carry out another attack in the hospital but Dawood Ibrahim did not approve of it and asked him to flee the country. In Dubai, another man was getting even more restless. The fact that Chhota Rajan would plot a revenge and his name would crop up was giving Rai sleepless nights.

Almost fifteen years after the daring attack on Chhota Rajan, when I visited the plush Sawan Court, residents clearly remembered the gunshots. The story of the attack had been passed on to the various members of the Thai-Indian families who stayed within the complex. After

Chhota Rajan was arrested from Indonesia in 2015, the Sawan Court residents spoke of the deadly attack. 'We never knew a don was living amidst us,' one of the residents told me. My story headlined 'Indians in Bangkok tell tales of don who lived in their midst' was published in *Mumbai Mirror* on 4 November 2015.

18

Nana's Revenge on Annas

The Thai police had deployed heavy security at Samitivej Hospital. Half a dozen policemen secured the floor on which Chhota Rajan was admitted in anticipation of a second attack.

When Chhota Rajan regained consciousness and opened his eyes, he got extremely angry. He couldn't care less that he had survived the attack. He tried to yank out the intravenous drip and get out of his bed. But he reeled under the pain of his wounded abdomen. Slowly, as the effect of the anaesthesia wore off, Chhota Rajan started recalling the deadly attack on his life. The thought that his rival Dawood Ibrahim had managed to track him down to Bangkok and had even planned an attack left him furious and shaken. He desperately wanted to know who the rat was.

Chhota Rajan summoned his trusted aide Santosh Shetty to the hospital. At first, he had suspected that

Santosh Shetty was involved in the attack but he then decided to call him anyway and gauge his reaction. The attack reeked of Dawood Ibrahim and Chhota Shakeel. But he wanted to snuff out the meddlers and make them pay for it.

'Who was it? Find out who it was!' Rajan yelled, drawing the attention of the medical staff in his room. Santosh Shetty assured him that he would get down to finding out the mole immediately.

Brought up in the plush Breach Candy area of South Mumbai, Santosh Shetty had studied hotel management to join his family's eatery business. But soon after he joined his father at work, they started having regular fights. The differences kept him away from home and eventually led him into bad company. He started smuggling gold and electronics to make a living. He graduated to smuggling drugs from South Africa, before landing in Nashik jail. After his release, Santosh Shetty chose to settle down in Bangkok. Though they had done business dealings before, it was in the Thai capital that he grew closer to Chhota Rajan.

Santosh Shetty's main responsibility now was to whisk away Chhota Rajan from the hospital and then from Thailand. But for that, Chhota Rajan needed to recover completely. Meanwhile, he put his entire force and every contact to trace the men behind the attack. It also struck them that besides Chhota Rajan's close family members, only one of their hotelier friends from Mumbai, Vinod Shetty, knew about his whereabouts. Vinod Shetty ran a bar in a western suburb of Mumbai that he owned in partnership with Satish Hegde. Santosh Shetty grew suspicious of Vinod Shetty but he did not want to jump to any conclusion and harm a member of his community without enough evidence. He coaxed his sources to find out more. Soon it turned out that Vinod Shetty had switched sides and now owed allegiance to Sharad Anna. Santosh Shetty could not establish why and how Vinod Shetty had passed on the information, but his association with Sharad Anna was enough to make him a suspect. Chhota Rajan fumed when he heard about Vinod Shetty and instantly ordered a hit. On 2 November 2000, a little over a month after the attack on Chhota Rajan, a man named Fakira Shetty called up Vinod Shetty on the pretext of passing on some information and money that Chhota Rajan had sent for him. An unsuspecting Vinod Shetty agreed to meet him at Titan Bar in Panvel.

Vinod Shetty left for Panvel accompanied by his business partners Satish Hegde and Shankar Iyer. His driver Mohammad Shakil drove them to Mumbai's satellite extension. At Titan Bar, they met Fakira Shetty and two of his friends and sat down for drinks and food. Fakira Shetty got up after a while and asked Vinod Shetty to follow him in his car, which the latter agreed to. Fakira Shetty abruptly halted at a point on the Uran–Panvel road near Chinchpada. Suddenly, it dawned on Vinod Shetty that something was amiss. Satish Hegde and he walked towards Fakira Shetty to ask him about the abrupt halt. But before they could say anything, Fakira Shetty turned around and shot Vinod Shetty. Satish Hegde jumped into some bushes and managed to save his life. Iyer and Shakil were also shot dead. The news of the triple murder shook Mumbai and the tremors were felt till Dubai. Chhota Rajan had made a major comeback. His next target would be Sharad Anna and then he would go after the smaller players, he thought. Santosh Shetty assured him of all help, but first he would have to escape from the clutches of the Thai police. Mumbai Police wanted to get Chhota Rajan extradited after the triple murder in Panvel and had started communicating with the Thai and Indian authorities.

But before anyone could close in on Chhota Rajan, he escaped from the hospital on 24 November with the help of the Thai military. The local police only found two long ropes dangling from his window after his daring escape. They also found some trekking equipment but the thought of a short, plump, injured man descending from a room at such height just did not add up. Santosh Shetty had pulled some strings and got the Thai military to rescue Chhota Rajan. He sneaked out Chhota Rajan into a military vehicle parked in the hospital's compound and got the men to drive him to the Thailand–Cambodia border. From there, Chhota Rajan was airlifted to a safe place in Siem Reap. After spending a few weeks at leisure in Cambodia, Chhota Rajan left for Tehran where Santosh Shetty and his other punters, Bharat Nepali and Bunty Pandey, joined him. Chhota Rajan was looked after by a Muslim caretaker, who nursed him for several months. He fell in love with the woman, who went on to bear his son.

* * *

Back in Dubai, Rai was restless. He knew that sooner or later Chhota Rajan would discover his role. A devotee of Mahalingeshwara, Rai had taken to praying to the deity every morning for an hour, a practice he continues to date. To divert his mind from Chhota Rajan, Rai focused on Bengaluru, a city that was now witnessing a real estate boom. The number of brokers in the city had multiplied, so had the offices of real-estate developers. Every ten to fifteen kilometres, one could see a building under construction.

One such prime property on Cunningham Road had gone into dispute after two claimants decided to purchase the same piece of land. One of them was a realtor named Subbaraju. A number of civil suits were filed till one day Subbaraju received a threatening call from Dubai, advising him to settle amicably. He was warned of dire consequences if he failed to pay heed to the advice. But the realtor did not take the threat seriously and refused to reach an agreement.

On 5 January 2001, at around 5.30 p.m., Subbaraju was sitting in his office at Seshadripuram Main Road when two men suddenly barged in, even as the watchman tried to stop them. Before Subbaraju could respond, they fired two rounds. One bullet hit his forehead while the other pierced through his chest. He collapsed instantly. The attackers ran out of the office and towards Swastik Circle. There, they boarded an autorickshaw and headed towards Anandrao Circle. Subbaraju's son Jagdish, who was outside the office when his father was shot at, started chasing the attackers. On the way, he informed a constable and both of them started chasing the attackers. But the men brandished their revolvers at Jagdish and the constable and told them to stop following. The men got off at Anandrao Circle and began running towards Kapali Theatre. A mobile phone slipped out of the pocket of one of the men. The constable immediately picked up the phone but the attackers managed to escape.

Subbaraju was rushed to Mallige Hospital where he was declared 'brought dead'. The police began investigating the case and identified one of the shooters as Yusuf Suleiman Qadri alias Yusuf Bachkana, a dreaded killer from the Chhota Rajan gang who had now switched loyalties to Ravi Poojary and Guru Satam. But before the investigation was completed, Rai admitted to have committed the crime in a sensational interview that appeared in the Kannada tabloid *Hi Bangalore*. He openly confessed that he was behind Subbaraju's murder.

Rai's terror had once again gripped the city. A few weeks after the realtor's murder, Rai called up his arch-rival Sreedhar. The two shared a bittersweet relationship by now and Rai was keen to gauge Sreedhar's reaction.

'See, Sreedhar, Subbaraju has been killed,' Rai said in one breath as soon as Sreedhar picked up the phone.

'Aren't you ashamed of yourself? I don't give a damn about you!' Sreedhar said. 'You are a rat hiding in a hole. If you have the guts, come and face me here in Bengaluru.'

'Where is this confidence coming from, Sreedhar? How dare you speak to me like this?' Rai raised his voice.

After a briefly bitter conversation, the two dons went on to discuss Bengaluru city, their children and how Sreedhar's white-collar work was shaping up. They spoke for four hours.

Rai knew that it was time for him to return and reclaim his kingdom. The threat from Chhota Rajan was looming large and he did not want to take a chance. He knew that an extradition treaty had been signed between India and the United Arab Emirates that could give the Karnataka Police an upper hand in getting all the law-breakers back home for legal action. The CBI had already issued a red-corner notice against him. His mind raced on how and when he could get back to Bengaluru.

19

Dubai to Dungeon

The opulence of the Dubai International Airport can leave one wide-eyed. Spread over 7000 acres, the busiest airport in the world boasts of shiny pathways with date trees on either side, Zen gardens and the world's top brands to shop from. But everything takes a back seat when the prying eyes of officials at the security and immigration checkpoints scrutinize passengers. A document here and there and one may end up being whisked away by officials to a corner for questioning. Given that nearly 80 million travellers arrive and depart from the airport every year, the security system needs to be top-notch and extra vigilant.

But when Rai walked into Dubai airport on 14 May 2002, he was extraordinarily calm. The fake passport that he was carrying did not bother him one bit. In the passport, he was Dolphy R. Joseph Rego, a resident of Narayana Nagar, near Nehru Centre, AB Road, Mumbai

400018. A driving licence too, which was found on him, mentioned the same name and address. Rai was caught as soon as he flashed the fake passport to the airport officials and was later handed over to the Dubai Police. But he remained composed. His calm demeanour was in all probability a part of his plan to stage an arrest to get back to Bengaluru. He preferred to be in a jail rather than in the open air in Dubai where he could be attacked anytime. Within a week after his arrest in Dubai, Rai was brought to Bengaluru. A team consisting of police inspector S.K. Umesh and DCP Ravindra Prasad, the Interpol and CBI officers was sent to Dubai to identify Rai and arrest him. From Dubai, he was first taken to the CBI headquarters in New Delhi where he was interrogated for a day. He was then taken for interrogation at CBI, Bengaluru, and then to the High Grounds Police Station.

Rai's contacts were such that even before the team reached Dubai, he knew about their arrival. According to Umesh, the CBI and the Interpol had information that Rai had met Dawood Ibrahim. He was quizzed for several hours before being sent to Bengaluru.

Media persons had gathered outside Bengaluru airport when Rai was brought out handcuffed. The don smiled calmly at everyone and posed for pictures. He waved and greeted everyone with folded hands like a celebrity before being put in a police van, which was chased by photographers and news channels. The Bengaluru Police took pride in their achievement.

'Dawood Ibrahim aide and Karnataka's most wanted criminal Muthappa Rai was handed over by Dubai authorities to the Bengaluru police team on Wednesday,' read a *Times of India* report. 'Reacting to Rai's arrest in Dubai, Police Commissioner H.T. Sangliana got in touch with the CBI Director and through him alerted the Interpol for seeking Rai's deportation. He also got in touch with the Indian Embassy in UAE and requested them to prevail upon the Dubai Police to send Rai back. A request from Bengaluru police to extradite Rai is pending with Dubai Police since 1997,' the report added.

Rai had more than twenty cases, including four murder charges, registered against him. If the police investigations were fool proof and the witnesses assured, Rai would be staring at a lifetime in jail.

Several theories did the rounds after Rai's arrival. The foremost being that the Research and Analysis Wing (RAW), India's intelligence agency, had offered him a safety package in exchange of 'important information'. Another theory revolved around Rai's fallout with Sharad Anna. With no safety roof above his head, he found it better to return to his homeland where he would be less vulnerable.

An article in *Frontline* in 2002 stated, 'According to informed sources, RAW, which has "used" Chhota Rajan to get information on Dawood's activities, may also have had a hand in the deportation of Rai and might now want to "use" Rai.'

A few years later, Rai's close aide went on to attest this information in a news article that was published in *Talk* magazine. B.N. Jagadish, state president of an organization Rai had formed, was quoted saying, 'What do you know about Muthappa Rai? He has been ensuring the safety of the country by helping RAW. He provides them with intelligence inputs to help secure the nation.'

Chhota Rajan had now turned his focus on Sharad Anna. He had a long history with Sharad Anna as the latter had refused all his offers to join his camp. Instead, he had preferred to be in D-Company. Chhota Rajan got Santosh Shetty to send four men to Dubai to keep a close watch on Sharad Anna. The four shooters—Karan Singh, Manoj Kotian, Vimal Kumar and a Nepali called Amar Bam—were given weapons and asked to wait for the right opportunity to strike. For more than a week the assassins closely followed Sharad Shetty everywhere. With a chain of hotels and restaurants that he had acquired, Sharad Anna would hop from one meeting to another. One of his most regular hang-outs was the posh India Club at the Oud Metha locality in Dubai. Chhota Rajan's team decided to attack him in this club.

One of the gang members, Manoj Kotian, who could speak in Kannada, befriended Sharad Anna at the club that was frequented by several Indian businessmen and diplomats. Kotian too had posed as an Indian businessman. On 19 January 2003, when Sharad Shetty walked out of the club casually chatting with Kotian, two men opened fire at him. The sharpshooters shot him in the head, leaving no chance of survival. He died on the spot as the trio fled. The news of Sharad Anna's death was flashed prominently in Dubai, Mumbai and Bengaluru—all three cities with a common thread, that of gangsters.

'Indians shocked over Sharad Shetty's killing', ran a headline in Gulf News.

'Dawood aide Sharad Shetty killed in Dubai,' said Rediff.com

Chhota Rajan was elated. He jumped with joy and let out a hearty laugh when the news was conveyed to him. But his revenge was far from over. He wanted to track down the other meddlers and kill them as well.

20

Bengaluru Mafia Goes Legit

A sudden placidity engulfed Bengaluru's underworld. As Rai cooled his heels behind bars, Sreedhar was on a new high, trying to establish himself as a clean man with white-collar businesses. His weekly tabloid *Agni* was reaching out to over 5000 people. While some compared it to Jayaraj's *Garibi Hatavo* that Sreedhar called a 'rag', others believed that *Agni* mimicked the format of *Lankesh Patrike*, a popular Kannada tabloid that focused on culture, philosophy, literature and progressive thoughts. At its peak, *Lankesh Patrike* sold over 3.5 lakh copies. In 1995, the tabloid culture of Bengaluru took a swift turn with the launch of a sensational newspaper called *Hi Bangalore*. Started by a journalist named Ravi Belagere, the unique format of the tabloid was an instant hit among those who enjoyed scandals and crime peppered with sleaze. Belagere, who had a short tryst with *Lankesh Patrike* as a crime writer, had very good contacts in the underworld. When he came up with the idea of starting his own paper, Sreedhar claimed to be the one who backed him. He even credits himself for coming up with the name 'Hi Bangalore' as the one Belagere had in mind—Hello Bangalore—was already registered.

Hi Bangalore garnered a massive readership within a short period of time by exposing scandals on film stars and politicians, doing stories on escorts, pimps, prostitutes, godmen and also by romanticizing criminals. In just about a year, the weekly tabloid was selling about one lakh copies. And with the increased circulation, Belagere too enjoyed a sudden fame, making him an influential figure in publishing circles. Sreedhar, who had backed him at first, felt neglected.

Sreedhar, with his carefully cultivated image, was tired of Belagere's glorification of the underworld. He would address the criminals as Tiger and Cheetah in his news reports, exalting the outlaws instead of bringing them to book. To deviate from this glorified narrative of criminals, the now-reformed don established *Agni* in 1998.

Hi Bangalore, however, continued to lead the Kannada tabloid market in Bengaluru. Then came a big-ticket interview with none other than Rai, who was holed up in Dubai at that time. In June 2000, Belagere travelled all the way to Dubai to meet Rai. The first of the three-part interview was flashed on the front page of *Hi Bangalore* on 30 June 2000. The headline said:

'Dubai: *Innenda Muthappa Rai*? (Dubai: What did Muthappa Rai say?)'

'*Ondu Rochaka Mukhamukhi*. (A sensational face-to-face encounter.)'

The article introduced Rai as the man who was addressed as Anna by none other than Dawood Ibrahim and Sharad Shetty. In Dubai circles, he was known as NM Rai, owner of two nightclubs, a software company in partnership with an Arab, a bungalow, several cars and having a penchant for horse racing. The interview made sensational revelations on how Rai pulled the trigger on four people sitting in Dubai. The don went on to confess the killings of Jayaraj, Oil Kumar and timber merchant Robert D'Silva. The last one had earned him Rs 15 crore, the don boasted.

'I killed Jayaraj with a 12-bore gun. That was the first time I had come face to face with the don. Two hours after the murder, I was in Windsor Manor Hotel. I called Oil Kumar to tell him that I had kept my promise and after that, jumped into the pool for a swim,' Rai stated nonchalantly. 'I had first planned to eliminate Jayaraj in his house. But it was like a fortress. So we made another plan,' he said. Rai went on to affirm that Bengaluru murders and Dubai telephones have a long connection. When Belagere asked the don if he would ever leave Dubai, he said, 'I left Puttur, I left Bengaluru, why won't I leave Dubai? I have left India only temporarily. DCP Kempaiah was responsible for my exit. His men planted the explosives in my farmhouse. But Bengaluru will always hear my voice.'

Hi Bangalore sold like hot cakes after Rai's interview was flashed on the front page. This wasn't, however, his first interview to the media. Although he had earlier spoken to many Kannada newspapers, this one clearly stood out. This made *Hi Bangalore* the leading tabloid while *Agni* simply continued to remain afloat. Sreedhar refrained from sensationalism and tried his best to don an intellectual image. *Agni* focused on columns by progressive writers and small-time poets on issues such as farmers' troubles and Dalit struggles. But Sreedhar soon realized the need to revisit his past to retain his readership.

He started a column called 'Dadagiriya Dinagalu', where he wrote about his days in the underworld. His writings, which chronicled his life, attracted the attention of readers with an inclination for crime stories. Though his paper didn't manage to break the circulation figures, the editor's tag worked for Sreedhar. He would hobnob in literary circles, something he had longed for and cherished immensely. It is through these circles that the idea of starting a pro-Kannada organization took shape in his mind. Sreedhar announced an outfit that would stand for the Kannadigas's pride: Karunada Sene. Launched amidst much fanfare, Karunada Sene was inaugurated by matinee superstar Rajkumar. President of the Kannada Sahitya Parishat Chandrashekhar Patil, well-known Kannada writer Baraguru Ramachandrappa, Dalit Sangharsa Samiti leader Indudhara Honnapura, farmer leader K.S. Puttannaiah and Bengaluru's most sought-after criminal lawyer, C.H. Hanumantharaya, were among the guests at the launch of Sreedhar's organization. Many thought that Sreedhar's Karunada Sene was modelled on

Bal Thackeray Shiv Sena to cash in on the 'Karnataka for Kannadigas' movement that was brewing within all sections of society. The *Telegraph* reported:

> The motto of the Karunada Sene is simple: when in Karnataka, be a Kannadiga. The group was set up in Bengaluru last month, with the avowed goal of 'getting Bengaluru back from the multinationals and outsiders'. Founder-member Agni Shridhar stresses that the group has chalked out its agenda, which begins with the language issue. Among other things, the Karunada Sene wants Kannada to be spoken in all public places, only Kannada films to be screened and Kannada to be made the medium of instruction in primary schools. In its next stage, the organisation says it is going to focus on employment: demanding that locals be given a preference in jobs and local industry, a protected status. The Karunada Sene's fight—for the time being—is against Hindi. In step two, it plans to take on English.

Sreedhar was thrilled with the response he received. With a new-found confidence, he dabbled in one creative field after another. He next set his sights on film-making. In between, he published a compilation of his columns in a three-volume book, using the title of his column: *Dadagiriya Dinagalu*. The book won him the Karnataka State Sahitya Akademi Award and was even translated into English under the title 'My Days in the Underworld'. Sreedhar then began scripting for a film from a chapter of his book. The events leading up to Kotwal's murder were made into a movie titled *Aa Dinagalu* in 2007, directed by K.M. Chaitanya and music by the illustrious Ilayaraja. Sreedhar's character was played by the critically acclaimed actor Atul Kulkarni. The good reviews that *Aa Dinagalu* garnered rekindled Sreedhar's interest in the film industry. He spent the next few years immersed in scriptwriting and produced five more Kannada films: *Kallara Santhe*, *Thamassu*, *Edegarike*, *Kiragoorina Gayyaligalu* and *Slum Bala*. Each one of his films drew parallels from the crime world that the ex-don had experienced first-hand.

From an underworld don to an editor, writer and film-maker, Sreedhar's journey had been extremely dynamic. But intellectual stimulation was not enough to keep him financially satisfied. He began to expand his territory across Bengaluru's real estate market, which was growing exponentially. The city had grown to become the tech capital of India with multinational IT firms, call centres and banks setting up their head offices there. Land was valuable in Bengaluru but most of it was under litigation by the new generation who fought over their ancestral properties. Real estate sharks would find it difficult to deal with sparring co-owners or wait till the overburdened Indian courts settled disputes. That is when the land mafia stepped in.

'My bread and butter comes from real estate. I have not cheated anyone. I am very thorough in documentation. My main source of money is through real estate. Films and cultural initiatives are secondary,' Sreedhar maintains.

Sreedhar and his minions would mediate between two parties and settle land disputes. In return, a fixed sum would be handed over to them. A Bengalurean who has closely observed Sreedhar's dealings narrates an incident when a close associate of Sreedhar met a renowned writer at a function. She told him that a very big fan of his wanted to meet him and had sent a car for him. The Kannada writer, who had some time to spare, agreed to hop on. The car stopped at Sreedhar's gated residence in ISRO Layout. After a brief interaction, Sreedhar came to the point. He had found an open plot of land in Hanumantha Nagar, which turned out to be in the name of the writer's deceased father. Sreedhar offered him Rs 1,00,001 as a token amount to let him sell off the open plot and handle the deals. The writer politely turned down his offer and left. But not everyone had that kind of integrity. A large number of people who were entangled in land disputes approached Sreedhar instead of the police or the judiciary. Sreedhar and his gang would first use their clout to get the work done, but in case they had to deal with a tough nut, *chaku-churis* (arms) came out without much thought.

* * *

Sreedhar's house stands on a sprawling piece of land that also houses the *Agni* office. The high iron gates have a tiny square window through which a guard peeps out and after a basic scrutiny, lets you in. Inside, a few cars are parked. About half a dozen, well-built men guard his main door. His critics often joke about how his security guards are paid more than his journalists.

Sreedhar mostly meets his visitors on the first floor of his bungalow. The living room contains a massive library stacked with spiritual and esoteric literature comprising books by Osho, Manto, Paulo Coelho, among others. A grandfather now, Sreedhar keeps his family members away from the prying eyes of the media. Bachchan still faithfully shadows Sreedhar everywhere. When I met Sreedhar, he was busy with the relaunch of Karunada Sene, an organization he had created and then ignored for a long time.

'We are planning a grand relaunch,' he said while checking posters and other literature meant for the event.

On 16 July 2016, close to a thousand people gathered at Sir Puttanna Chetty Town Hall to cheer for Sreedhar. The relaunch of his Karunada Sene threw Bengaluru's traffic out of control. All active members of the organization were seated on the dais. They stood up, one after the other, to address the audience. But when K. Sunil Kumar, the organization's working president, rose to talk, the crowd erupted enthusiastically. They cheered, whistled and clapped for the leader, who smiled pleasantly at them and stood in silence till his fans allowed him to talk.

'Your support means a lot to me,' he said after another round of applause.

Dressed in crisp white, Sunil Kumar looked like a suave politician, who aimed at a progressive future for Bengaluru. But where did Sreedhar find this man who enjoyed such a huge following?

Sunil Kumar went by the alias Silent Sunila. A notorious rowdy, Silent Sunila had grown up in Gayatri

Nagar where he took to crime at the age of fifteen. He shot to notoriety after he murdered a policeman and was sent to a remand home as a juvenile. Silent Sunila came to be known in the underworld circles of Bengaluru by his nickname that he had earned owing to his reserved nature. Sreedhar claimed that the gangster had approached him saying he didn't want to indulge in petty crimes and only wanted to deal with the sharks of the crime world.

'He had offers to join the Mumbai and Dubai underworld. But he chose to come to me,' said Sreedhar. 'He hardly talks. He only grasps. He will sit like a Buddha in front of you. Sunila has another alias, Amul Baby,' Sreedhar said with a hint of pride over his protégé. Women adored Sunila's innocent-looking face and had come up with the nickname Amul Baby. Sreedhar was in the process of scripting a movie on Silent Sunila with the same title and had roped in director Duniya Soori for it. Soori wanted Silent Sunila to play himself and even went on to make a short trailer for the film. But the project was put on the back burner as Sreedhar and Sunila focused on other priorities. But some said that Sunila's fast-expanding waistline was responsible for the project being put on hold.

Sreedhar's rebooted version of Karunada Sene has drastically changed its tone to appeal to the masses. From its 'Karnataka for Kannadigas' motto, Sreedhar now has a progressive viewpoint. 'Be it a Tamilian or a Marathi, everyone is welcome in Karnataka. They should be treated with respect. They are our guests,' the former don now preaches. Though he is not sure whether the organization aims to get into politics full-fledgedly, he is in the process of forming a women's wing of the Sene called Karunada Mahila Pade. The don is also grooming a few women to demand equal rights in a political party or start their own party instead.

'Why should women play second fiddle? They need to take centre stage,' he tells his members.

Sreedhar says that the motto of Karunada Sene is not to segregate people on the basis of language and caste, but to wage a war against the drug culture that is ruining the lives of youngsters. When Karnataka and Tamil Nadu were at loggerheads over the Supreme Court's order to release the Cauvery river water to Tamil Nadu, Karunada Sene members were among the thousands of protesters. Sreedhar is positive that in the coming years the Sene will be a force to reckon with in Karnataka.

For the former don, this was his trump card to keep himself relevant on the social front.

21

Rai Back to Rule the Roost

Twenty-two months of incarceration, a dozen cases, four murder charges, and finally acquittal from all of them. When Rai was deported from Dubai, his advocate Tomy Sebastian confidently stated in the *Frontline* article of 2002, 'If the Karnataka government sets up a special court to try [as it has been saying] him [Rai], I will have him out in three months.' Sebastian's confidence in getting his client out despite him being charged under stringent sections like 302 (murder), and 120B (conspiracy) of the IPC, the Arms Act and the Explosive Substances Act, was remarkable.

On 16 April 2004, when Rai stepped out of the Parappana Agrahara Central Prison, over hundred cars blocked the Bengaluru–Hosur road to receive their anna. They cheered and showered him with garlands as he walked out, hands folded. His wife Reca was waiting for him in the car, which took the couple to an undisclosed location. During interrogations, Rai proved to be a tough nut to crack. He was grilled about his connections with Dawood Ibrahim, Sharad Anna and others in India, but he did not disclose any names that could lead to further arrests. After stepping out of jail, Rai was free from legal tangles, but he was well aware that the danger from the underworld was still lurking. He had enemies in Bengaluru, Mangaluru and even abroad.

During his jail time, the don had decided on one thing: he would live a reformed life henceforth. Once he stepped out of prison, he remained true to his decision. People close to him would say that Muthappa Anna had only Rs 1 crore when he was deported, but few knew that he was a shrewd investor. Predicting that a real estate boom was round the corner, Rai bought 100 acres of disputed land in Bidadi, thirty-five kilometres from Bengaluru, on the Mysore expressway. He started making substantial money by selling tiny pockets from the sprawling area. In one such deal, he managed to sell a portion of land for Rs 3 crore per acre that he had procured for just Rs 4 lakh per acre. He also used a vast portion of the land to construct a mansion for himself. A golf cart is used to ferry visitors from the gate to the main entrance of the bungalow. He bought a Land Cruiser that is custom-made to protect him from any kind of attack. The German-designed bomb- and bullet-proof vehicle can withstand AK-47 bullets and grenade attacks. While his contemporary Sreedhar made a foray into print journalism, Rai bought a large stake in one of the topmost Kannada channels but chose to remain a silent partner. He dedicated most of his time to land deals. In 2005, a senior lawyer from the city took up a pro bono case of a school for the blind, located on a prime plot in Whitefield. As the locality developed as a tech hub, prices soared and caught the attention of the land mafia. Some of the school's trustees, allegedly hand in glove with the mafia, planned to sell off the land. The lawyer put the best of his staff on the job to unearth information and documents that would help him save the blind children's school. Suddenly one day, the lawyer got a call from Rai who requested a meeting with him. The lawyer instead sent one of his men to meet the don. Rai politely placed a proposal in front of them.

'Leave this tiny piece of land. It is just nine acres. I will give you 100 acres on the outskirts of the city and even get the new school built for the children,' he offered.

The man returned and reported the offer made by Rai. But the lawyer didn't pay heed to it. Rai called again.

'Sir, I want to help the children,' he told the lawyer.

'To cheat the blind, one does not need any courage. It is sheer shamelessness,' the lawyer retorted.

'I have my own pressures to deal with. You have to understand,' he said.

'Ten men like you can make this country a heaven,' the lawyer said sarcastically.

Rai laughed and thanked him for the compliment. The lawyer continued to fight the case.

After finding a foothold in the city once again, Rai decided to concentrate on his social makeover. In 2008, he launched Jaya Karnataka, a social organization that took shape in his mind while he was incarcerated.

He defines Jaya Karnataka as a not-for-profit, democratic and non-political organization, aimed at improving the quality of life of the people of Karnataka. Its vision and mission have been criticized by social activists who couldn't believe that a former don was now talking about matching up with the greatness of Basava, Ambedkar and their likes. Jaya Karnataka's vision statement reads:

An effort for equality. An aim to end corruption. Working towards a goal to form a new model State as per the dreams of Buddha, Basava, Ambedkar, and KuVemPu. Protest to demand supporting price for the crops grown by farmers. An honest effort to bring the State minorities to mainstream. Fight against harassment of women. A goal to attain social justice to the Dalits and Backwards. An effort to make India prosperous as per the dreams of Dr APJ Abdul Kalam. A never ending protest to protect Kannada State and its language from any constraints. All Kannadigas in Karnataka are Emperors! And those residing in Kannada land are Kannadigas. There is only one land. The natural resources like water, forest and environment on our land should be protected and has to be passed to the next generation. As per the words of Swami Vivekananda, an effort has to be made to convert the young students as new architects of Karnataka. Let Mother Teresa's Social Work and Selflessness be our ideology. An effort to make Kannadigas lead a simpler life.

His larger-than-life persona and authority over the city worked well for Jaya Karnataka. It rapidly gained popularity and boasts of 700 branches across the city today. Like the Chaluvaligars who had taken to the streets, Rai's men also led protests on the roads against the sharing of the Cauvery water with Tamil Nadu. The former don also invested in other initiatives such as cleaning up Bengaluru following Prime Minister Narendra Modi's call for Swachh Bharat (Clean India) and a project called 'Water for All', through which the don plans on supplying water for Re 1 a bucket.

Even though their organizations have parallel goals, Rai and Sreedhar don't cross each other's paths any more. Both in their sixties now, the ageing dons have their areas demarcated. Sreedhar has an army of rowdy-sheeters, some of whom are key members in the Karunada Sene. Silent Sunila, Onte Rohit, Mulama Lokesh and others mainly manage his operations.

Rai has his army of Bunts. It is said that the dons have reached an understanding over the land deals—while Sreedhar mostly operates within Bengaluru, Rai has spread his wings outside the city.

Epilogue

Meeting Rai

As you walk down the ninth street of tony Sadashivanagar, the posh bungalows nestled amidst a dense thicket are telling of the socio-economic status of the residents. A large poster featuring faces of activists hangs from a tree next to a high-rise, a jarring blot on the otherwise idyllic setting of the building. The high-rise is Raj Mahal, one of Rai's many houses in Bengaluru.

Half a dozen armed guards with walkie-talkies and holstered guns crowd around the entrance of the building. As I plonk myself down on a chair next to the entrance, waiting to be summoned upstairs, I can't take my eyes off the monstrosity of an SUV parked next to me—one of Rai's many wheels.

'It is anna's,' says one of the hefty men when he finds me staring at the car. Natives of Azamgarh in Uttar Pradesh, the guards are tasked with rallying around Rai 24x7. They stay in the same building in special quarters allocated to them. And when Rai chooses to stay in his large mansion in Bidadi, the guards follow him as part of a burgeoning entourage.

About fifteen minutes later, the walkie-talkie of one of the men crackles into life. A guard clad in a grey safari suit gestures another to accompany me upstairs. The lift stops on the seventh floor and opens onto a swanky apartment. What appears to be the reception of a corporate office is actually a waiting room, furnished with a dark leather sofa set and a glass side table. That the owner of the apartment is a man of refined tastes is evident even from the wall clock hanging on an otherwise blank wall. It's a Rolex. Rai, dressed simply in a white shirt and trousers, walks into the room. Following months of correspondence, innumerable phone calls and text messages, referrals from journalists and police officers from both Mumbai and Bengaluru, I have finally managed to meet the man who was once India's most wanted criminal. At the top of the list of the most wanted perpetrators of crime in Bengaluru, a photograph of Rai holding a slate used to be displayed at most police stations.

The ruthless gangster, known for pulling the trigger without batting an eyelid, sat down in front of me. Had I been oblivious to his past, I would have assumed that he was a well-to-do Bunt businessman of Dakshin Kannada origin, who probably ran a chain of Udupi restaurants. Rai had a welcoming smile on his face, which helped defuse much of my anxiety. Rai was followed by his close friend from Vijaya Bank: Jayakar Shetty. They escorted me into a smaller cabin where he held his official meetings. But before I could ask him anything, I was warned by Jayakar Shetty. 'See, when you are writing a book, don't mention anything that would tarnish anna's hard-earned image. You have to be very careful,' he said. But Rai was much calmer and constantly smiling. His Hindi, though laced with a heavy south Indian accent, is reminiscent of his proximity with the Mumbai mafia.

'*Tumko main sab kahani batata tha. But tumhara kitab poora underworld ke baare mein hai. Mera toh sirf ek character hai. Poora book mere baare me hota toh main bolta.* (I would have told you my entire story. But your book is about the whole underworld. I am just a character in it. If it was entirely about me, I would have told you.)'

'*Arre baba, tum mera story likh dega toh mera picture me kya dikhayega?* (If you write my story, what will we show in my film?)'

He looks at me enquiringly to ascertain if I know anything about the movie *Rai*, which is a biopic on him, being made by Bollywood film-maker Ram Gopal Varma (RGV). The director known for his underworld-themed movies such as *Satya*, *Company* and *Sarkar*, is said to have researched about Rai and approached him with the proposal. Apparently, Kannada star Sudeep was to be cast as Rai but RGV rooted for his favourite actor Vivek Oberoi and even released a teaser to announce the film. The sixty-second-long video has Vivek Oberoi's face modelled on Rai's. RGV calls him the greatest gangster ever. The trailer plays out with the following super:

> It takes twenty years for a simple murder trial in India.
> He was acquitted in twenty murder cases in just twenty months. He started with Rs 30 in his pocket. And after a thirty-year criminal career, is now worth Rs 30,000 crore. History said, 'Crime doesn't pay.' He proved that crime pays. Then why is he worshipped today? By lakhs and lakhs of people. Rai—the greatest gangster ever.

RGV's obsession with Rai was put down in a *Bangalore Mirror* article that chronicled his tweets:

> Bengaluru underworld has a far more viscous quality which explains its pan-India effect and its links to the Mumbai- and Dubai-based underworld. Finally, I always thought Godfather was a fictional character but after meeting Muthappa Rai, I realized he is real and he is the father of all Godfathers. Muthappa Rai, I think, is the Bahubali of the Underworld. The research I gathered on Bengaluru underworld in general and on Muthappa Rai in particular came from multiple sources and not from Rai himself. What I heard about Muthappa Rai from others, including cops and his enemies, is far far more than what I actually heard from Mr Rai himself. After all the understanding I had of the underworld, I realized today that the D-Company pales in comparison to the B-Company.

Rai is visibly excited about being called the 'Godfather' and the 'Bahubali of the Underworld'. Gushing over his upcoming venture, he gets a bit candid.

'I am a man for justice,' he announces.

'I have not earned a single penny in the underworld. This Sreedhar, Bachchan and others, I have seen them all. They were all below me. But they were after the money. I never ran after the money.

'I cannot stand any kind of injustice. I will always be at the forefront for the needy. I was always a leader. Be it in school or in sports.

'You tell me jump from this high wall, I will do it. It is to show my courage. Even when I started working, I was a leader.'

But how can one disregard the crimes and murders that he has committed?

'See, politicians and the police exploited me. They took help from me and then abandoned me. My courage became my problem.'

He goes on to narrate his role in the murders of Jayaraj and Oil Kumar and chronicles his life through anecdotes that keep me at the edge of the seat.

If he never earned any money in the underworld, where does the wealth come from?

'I have a great deal of real estate. We had a large piece of land in my village as well. Now I am into the real estate business,' he says.

'I am not a bad man. I help everyone. I started my social organization to bring out the good side in me.'

The former don owns around 1000 acres of land in and around Bengaluru. His possessions across Karnataka make him a billionaire. His 250-acre estate in the hill station of Sakleshpur in Hassan district is much talked about for its biodiversity. Rai nurtured the land by planting over 3 lakh trees and created a 15-acre artificial lake, which is said to house a rich and diverse marine life. The who's who of Bollywood, the Kannada film industry and even political heavyweights have holidayed in his estate. He shows me a video of actor Zayed Khan thanking him for the wonderful time he spent with his family at the estate that has five-star quarters for guests.

As I finish my first instalment of a long interview, he hands me an invite for his son's wedding reception.

* * *

On 19 December 2016, two days after hosting the grand wedding reception of his son, the sixty-three-year-old ex-don stunned everyone by getting married himself in a very low-key gathering at his residence in Bidadi. This is his second marriage. In 2013, the don suffered a huge setback when his wife Reca died of breast cancer at St Elizabeth Hospital in Singapore. His second wife, Anuradha, a widow with two minor children, is an entrepreneur, whom he befriended through his sister-in-law. After a year-long courtship, the don narrated his entire life's story to Anuradha before the couple decided to get married.

'It's tough to be alone. I would often feel lonely. I wanted a companion,' the don would tell his friends. Anuradha, forty-five, is eighteen years younger than Rai.

Rai's popularity in the crime world has always remained a notch higher than that of other Bengaluru mafia members because of his connections to the fugitive gangster Dawood Ibrahim, who has now been identified as a global terrorist. But given his clout among the influential and the notorious, why does Rai, who now claims to have renounced violence, need so much security?

'Chhota Rajan has taken an oath to kill me.'

'A twenty-rupee bullet, that's it. And someone will become a big shot after killing me. I am Muthappa Rai after all.'

Acknowledgements

From the moment I landed in Bengaluru to research for this book, retired super cop Lava Kumar helped me navigate through various channels and gather information that helped shape this manuscript. Apart from arming me with contacts, he also shared his valuable perspective on the crime scene prevalent in the city during the last half of the twentieth century.

That this book has meticulous details of recorded crimes and even those that are off the books has much to do with senior journalist R. Somanath's inputs. An authority on the nexus between Karnataka's underworld and politics, he assisted me at every step and was always just a phone call away.

I would also like to extend my gratitude to former cops and wonderful storytellers B.K. Shivaram and B.B. Ashok Kumar, who took time out of their busy schedules to narrate stories about Bengaluru's mafia. I am grateful to former top cop G.A. Bava for generously letting me access his library packed with bundles of documents, rowdy sheets and statements of several gangsters. I am also thankful to Bengaluru Police officers H.N. Venkatesha Prasanna and S.K. Umesh for sharing interesting and lesser-known facts about reported crimes and their back stories.

I am indebted to Maharashtra Police encounter specialists Prakash Bhandary and Pradeep Sharma, who provided pertinent sources in Bengaluru and Mangaluru that helped stitch this book together.

Two other journalists from Bengaluru helped me gain a perspective and also put me in touch with their sources. The first being dynamic journalist–activist Gauri Lankesh, who helped me see the stories in a completely different light. She was among the first few people I met in Bengaluru when I started researching for the book. After a brief conversation over the phone, I reached Rajarajeshwari Nagar late in the evening. I remember trying to locate her bungalow but not being able to find my way in the darkness. She walked out of the gate to see if she could spot my autorickshaw and then guided the driver to her house. Memories of that night flashed in front of my eyes as television channels reported about her brutal murder on 5 September 2017. They repeatedly showed images of the poorly lit alley and how it had become a major obstacle in nabbing Gauri's killers. She had warmly hosted me and chatted for hours, giving me a picture of the city's black, white and grey shades. Though she had known me for only a few hours, she offered me to spend the night at her place without any hesitation. On several occasions, she guided me over the phone, providing clarity over many issues. Gauri, I wish you were here to read the final product.

The second being television journalist B. Narayan, who introduced me to several police officers and gangsters, and also sat with me during interviews, helping me with translations. Of the many people he introduced me to, was Sachiva Sridhar who walked me down Bengaluru's history and reflected on the 'Jayaraj–Kotwal zamana'.

My list would be incomplete without mentioning Urdu journalist Aziz Malik. He pulled several strings to organize interviews with some of the most important men in Bengaluru.

As a journalist, I learnt the most during my stint with *Mumbai Mirror*. I am truly grateful to my former editor Meenal Baghel for pushing me to deliver on my potential and beyond. Two other *Mumbai Mirror* colleagues who played a vital role in shaping this book are Harsh Vora, who combed through the first few chapters when I had barely managed to put down the first draft, and Amit Khosla, *Mumbai Mirror*'s national art editor, who is responsible for this book's striking cover. Thank you, Amit, for your creativity and the magical touch.

My heartfelt thanks to Lakshmi Govindrajan Javeri for giving momentum to this book.

At Penguin Random House India, I am truly grateful to my editor Milee Aishwarya for being patient through the various edits and keeping her faith in me throughout the journey. Her persistence drove me to comply with deadlines and deliver this project. My special thanks to

Indrani Dasgupta for reading and rereading my chapters and tightening the loose ends.

I would also like to thank Dr M.S. Shailaja for helping me with the Kannada translations. A big shout-out to my former boss and senior journalist B. Mahesh for providing important and relevant contacts in Bengaluru.

The most crucial contributions to this book have been made by three of my journalist friends. Sumitra Deb Roy of the *Times of India* who burnt the midnight oil along with me reading my drafts and editing them carefully. She has played a vital role in enhancing the narrative of this book. Kunal Guha from *Mumbai Mirror*, one of the finest writers I have known, took over parts of this book that were dull and made them interesting. Sayoni Sinha helped restructure the chapters and proofread every single one of them. I am truly grateful to you for making the book as error-free as possible.

If there is anything right with this book, the credit goes to none other than Hussain Zaidi. His understanding of the crime world and knack for storytelling is admirable. I was always a fan, but after our numerous sittings to discuss the chapters, the flow and the narrative of this book, my respect for him has grown immensely. I hope that I can continue to learn from him and am truly grateful that he offered me this opportunity.

References

Police dossiers and court documents were my main references.

The incidents and the anecdotes that weave the narrative together were made possible through personal interviews with reformed mafia members like Muthappa Rai, Agni Sreedhar and Tanveer. Several incidents mentioned in the book were shared by former underworld members, who had worked closely with various factions. However, many of their identities have not been revealed.

Family members of M.P. Jayaraj and Koli Faiyaz were of immense help. I conducted multiple rounds of interviews with several of them.

Former and current Bangalore Police officers provided a landmine of information, from files for research to interviews with individuals central to the book. Many of them spoke at length, helping me chronicle the most crucial events through personal interviews.

Some interesting aspects of the early history of Bangalore were sourced from M. Fazlul Hasan's

Bangalore Through the Centuries and writer Janaki Nair's essay titled 'Battles for Bangalore: Reterritorialising the City'.

Agni Sreedhar's exhaustive memoir *My Days in the Underworld: Rise of the Bangalore Mafia* was a great source to track the chronology of events.

S. Hussain Zaidi's path-breaking *Dongri to Dubai* and *Byculla to Bangkok* were my go-to books whenever I had to decipher the synergy between the Bengaluru and the Mumbai mafia.

I have referred to the archives of several newspapers such as the *Times of India*, *Bangalore Mirror*, *Deccan Herald*, *The Hindu*, *Indian Express*, etc., and some translations from Kannada newspapers *Hi Bangalore*, *Lankesh Patrike*, etc. I have also referred to websites like rediff.com and Indiakanoon.org.

Books:

Sreedhar, Agni. 2013. *My Days in the Underworld: Rise of the Bangalore Mafia*. Chennai: Tranquebar Press.

Hasan, M. Fazlul. 1970. *Bangalore Through the Centuries*. Bangalore: Historical Publications.

Zaidi, S. Hussain. 2012. *Dongri to Dubai*. New Delhi: Roli Books.

Zaidi, S. Hussain. 2014. *Byculla to Bangkok*. Noida: HarperCollins.

Articles:

'Prohibition cases'. *Deccan Herald*, 3 June 1955.

'2 con men caught, taken to police'. *Deccan Herald*, 5 March 1965.

Nair, Janaki. 'Battles for Bangalore: Reterritorialising the City'. Centre for the Study of Culture and Society, Bengaluru.

Chawla, Prabhu. 'The resignation drama'. *India Today*, 28 February 1986.

'Advocate shoots gangster'. *Times of India*, 13 April 1993.

Prasad, Srinivas. 'Mumbai mafia begins to flex muscle in Bangalore'. *Times of India*, 3 November 1997.

'Chhota Rajan aide killed in Bangalore'. *Times of India*, 8 November 1997.

Lulla, Anil Budur. 'Karnataka keeps a close watch on Mumbai's mafia'. *Times of India*, 2 August 1998.

Hande, Vikas. 'Reformed rowdies turn to real estate'. *Times of India*, 7 March 1999.

'Karnataka hopes to benefit from extradition treaty with UAE'. *Times of India*, 2 June 2000.

Balram, H.S. 'Stop Bangalore from becoming a sanctuary for criminals'. *Times of India*, 17 July 2000.

'Muthappa Rai played a major role in bid on Chhota Rajan's life'. *Times of India*, 8 March 2001.

'Law of the gun'. *Times of India*, 27 December 2001.

'Muthappa brought back to Karnataka'. *Times of India*, 31 May 2002.

'Rai brought gun culture to Bangalore'. *Times of India*, 31 May 2002.

Sharma, Ravi. 'Now, elusive evidence'. *Frontline*, June 22–July 5 2002.

'Sharad Shetty killed by two Rajan hitmen'. *Times of India*, 21 January 2003.

'Will Bangalore no longer be cosmo?' *Telegraph*, 19 December 2004.

Subramanya, K.V. 'The encounter that shook Bangalore'. *The Hindu*, 7 May 2005.

Chauhan, Bala. 'Don at dusk'. *Sunday Herald*, 22 October 2006.

'Muthappa Rai fears threat to life'. *The Hindu*, 29 September 2006.

Carney, Scott. 'The Godfather of Bangalore'. www.wired.com. 10 October 2008.

Srinivasaraju, Sugata. 'November regrets'. *Outlook*, 6 November 2008.

Nandakumar, Prathibha. 'Decoding Kannada Flag'. *Bangalore Mirror*, 2 November 2012.

Karnel, Savie. 'Who Hijacked the Language Cause?' Talkmag.in, 13 December 2012.

'Reopening of dance bars may lead to spurt in crime: Maharashtra police'. *DNA*, 16 July 2013.

Kumar, Praveen. 'Cubbon Police At It Again'. *Bangalore Mirror*. 25 May 2014.

Hazra, Aritra. 'Mumbai gangster Santosh Shetty opens up about Rajan, Dawood'. *Hindustan Times*. 13 October 2015.

George, T.J.S. 'How Liquor and Crime Shaped Bengaluru: An Excerpt From T.J.S. George's "Askew"'. *Caravan*, 3 November 2016.

Hemanth Kashyap and Chetan R. 'The godfather II'. *Bangalore Mirror*, 30 April 2016.

'I am at peace with people now. My past was not so: Muthappa Rai'. *Bangalore Mirror*, 30 April 2016.

Regional articles:

Somanath, R. 'Kotwalanna Mane Khaali Maadisidha Mune Gowda'. *Hi Bangalore*, 3 October 1997.

—. 'Avanobbaniddha Mune Gowda'. *Hi Bangalore*, 23 September 1997.

Belagere, Ravi. 'Matthe Muthappa Rai? Muthappa Rai Sandarshana'. *Hi Bangalore*, 11 July 1997.

Somanath, R. 'Layout Manjana Hathyeya Hindhe'. *Hi Bangalore*, 23 October 1998.

—. 'Tanveer's escape'. *Hi Bangalore*, 21 May 1999.

—. 'Sreedhar Sandarshana'. *Hi Bangalore*, 6 August 1999.

Belagere, Ravi. 'Dubai: Innenda Muthappa Rai'. *Hi Bangalore*, 30 June 2000.

—. 'Matthe Bharathakke Barutthene- Muthappa Rai'. *Hi Bangalore*, 7 July 2000.

—. 'Oil Kumarana Hendati Muthappa Raiyanna Keliddhenu'. *Hi Bangalore*, 14 July 2000.

Somanath, R. 'Builder Subbarajunannu Khodaye Galu Kollisidhare'. *Hi Bangalore*, 19 January 2001.

Belegere, Ravi. 'Builder Subbarajunannu Naane Kollisidhe'. *Hi Bangalore*, 19 January 2001.

—. 'Nannannu Sreedhar Kollabahudhu- Muthappa Rai Aatanka'. *Hi Bangalore*, 21 June 2002.

—. 'Rai Hathyege Yaaraskecchu? Bhugatalokadha pakka chukka' *Hi Bangalore*, 11 April 2003.

Somanath, R. 'Muthapppa Rai Mukha Mukhi'. *Lankesh Patrike*, 7 February 2003.

—. 'Nanna Thammanannu Rai Kollisidha- Yusuf Bachkana'. *Lankesh Patrike*, 23 November 2004.

—. 'Arasu Aasthige Muthappa Rai Kai'. *Lankesh Patrike*, 18 January 2005.

—. 'Revenge killing'. *Gauri Lankesh Vaarapatrike*, 23 September 2006.

—. 'Bengaluru Underworldge Naanu Kai Haakuvudilla Muthappa Rai'. *Gauri Lankesh Vaarapatrike*, 26 November 2012.

—. 'Amar Alvanannu Kollisiddhu Naanalla- Muthappa Rai'. *Gauri Lankesh Vaarapatrike*, 25 February 2013.

References to some incidents mentioned in the text:

Chapter 4, p. 36. 'The police squad . . . had testified', has been sourced from interviews with the police and some members of the underworld.

Chapter 11, pp. 106–107. The paragraph, 'As swords and machetes splattered . . . passed on the job to Kotwal', has been sourced from Agni Sreedhar's film *Aa Dinagalu* and his book *My Days in the Underworld*. It has been corroborated by former cop B.K. Shivaram in an interview.

Chapter 11. p. 107. The line, 'It turned out that Varada's father . . . to Kotwal', has been sourced from Agni Sreedhar's *My Days in the Underworld*.

Chapter 12, p. 122. The line, 'I don't want to . . . his future', has been sourced through from a personal interview with Agni Sreedhar.

Chapter 14, p. 142. The paragraph, 'Back in Bengaluru . . . I will kill Jayaraj', has been sourced from personal interview with Rai.

Chapter 14, p. 148. The line, 'Meanwhile, as a part of the larger . . . nuisance in a bar', has been sourced from *My Days in the Underworld* by Agni Sreedhar.

Chapter 15, p. 154. The paragraph, 'They rented a large house . . . meeting in Sadashivnagar', has been sourced through a personal interview with former cop B.K. Shivaram.

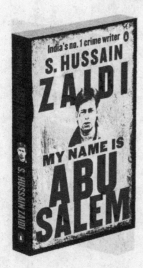

YOU MAY ALSO LIKE

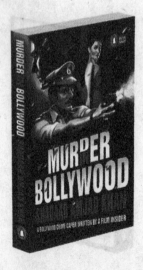

YOU MAY ALSO LIKE